THE GAMES
OF GOLF

THE GAMES
OF GOLF

DAVID RIHM

The Stephen Greene Press
Pelham Books

THE STEPHEN GREENE PRESS/PELHAM BOOKS

Published by the Penguin Group
Viking Penguin, a division of Penguin Books USA Inc., 375 Hudson Street,
    New York, New York 10014, U.S.A.
Penguin Books Ltd., 27 Wrights Lane, London W8 5TZ, England
Penguin Books Australia Ltd, Ringwood, Victoria, Australia
Penguin Books Canada Ltd, 2801 John Street, Markham, Ontario, Canada
    L3R 1B4
Penguin Books (N.Z.) Ltd, 182–190 Wairau Road, Auckland 10, New Zealand

Penguin Books Ltd, Registered Offices: Harmondsworth, Middlesex, England

First published in 1990 by The Stephen Greene Press/Pelham Books

Distributed by Viking Penguin, a division of Penguin Books USA Inc.

10 9 8 7 6 5 4 3 2

"Callaway System of Handicapping" by Lionel Callaway is reprinted by
permission.

Library of Congress Cataloging-in-Publication Data
Rihm, David.
    The games of golf / by David Rihm.
        p.   cm.
    "Pelham books,"
    ISBN 0-8289-0770-6
    1. Golf. I. Title.
    GV965.R54   1990
    796.352'3—dc 20   89-27079
                                CIP

Printed in the United States of America
Designed by Deborah Schneider
Set in Futura by CopyRight Inc., Bedford, MA
Produced by Unicorn Production Services, Inc.

To My Family
and especially my wife Bonnie,
who puts up with all the time I spend
in the game of golf.

CONTENTS

PART III
POINT COMPETITIONS   67

PART IV
SINGLE SHOT EVENTS AND OTHER GAMES   81

APPENDIX A
THE CALLAWAY SYSTEM OF HANDICAPPING   93

APPENDIX B
RULES OF GOLF: DIFFERENCES BETWEEN STROKE AND MATCH PLAY   97

FOREWORD

Most golfers play the game for a lot of different reasons, but probably the most common is for the competition: People love to test their mettle in an effort to come out on top—to win. Although competition in itself is exciting enough, sometimes you need a change of pace to keep things interesting (if a touring pro had to play the same course every week, he or she would certainly find it boring after awhile), and that's where this book comes in. Here, dozens of different competitive formats are clearly outlined and explained, from match play to stroke play; team play and individual play. No club pro should be without this guide, since it contains dozens of events that his or her club members will find fun and interesting. Likewise, casual golfers looking for ways to spice up their Saturday and Sunday mornings will do well to include this book among their bag of essentials.

As a veteran of 29 years on tour, most of my competitive experience has been spent laboring away at the most simple and straightforward of golf games, medal play, where the sum total of strokes taken over the course of a round or rounds is added up; the lowest score wins. Medal is truly the best way to determine who has played the best golf from the very beginning to the very end of the tournament. There's no doubt, however, that it is an unforgiving grind, since every hole counts, and a bad hole on the first day can come back to haunt you. That's why I've never thought of it as being a very good form of competition for casual players on a regular basis. You're out there to have fun, not earn a living, and believe me, there are many different games to be played that are a lot more enjoyable than the continuous grind of straight stroke play.

Probably the most popular form of competition on the amateur level is formally known as ''Four Ball Best Ball Match,'' which pits two two-player teams against each other in match play, with the better ball of each team counting as the score for that hole. Not only is it popular among amateurs, but it's also a favorite among touring pros—men, women, and seniors—during practice rounds. A variation of this game is Four Ball Best Ball Stroke, in which the better-ball score for a two-man team is added up and totaled after the specified number of holes have been completed. (It's the same format used for the Legends of Golf—the tournament that sparked today's Senior Tour.)

Team play is fun because of the feeling of camaraderie it promotes among partners. Several of the team games described in the text feature a twist that some amateurs may not have experienced: two players play the same ball, alternating shots. Talk about teamwork! This form of competition is still alive today among professionals in the Ryder Cup, where one day of the three-day matches is devoted to "Foursomes."

Another way to increase the fun of team play is to increase the size of the team—making all members of a foursome teammates—as in a Scramble, Pinehurst Foursomes, Chapman Foursomes, Best Ball or Two Best Balls of a Foursome.

Tired of counting strokes? Try a game like Stableford, Quota, or Bingle-Bangle-Bungle, which breaks performance down into points. For proof that this can be a refreshing change in how a tournament is contested, take a look at The International, now a regular event on the PGA Tour, where scoring is based on a modified Stableford system. Point games are fun because a bad hole or two won't knock you way out of the running, while a good hole or two can get you right back into the thick of things.

Some of these games aren't simply fun; they can also help you learn how to play better. Take "One Club," where a player is allowed to use only one club from tee to green, including holing out. I can't think of a better way for a golfer to learn or improve his or her shotmaking than to give them one club and send them out on the course to play nine or eighteen holes. Try it and you'll know what I mean the first time you face a short pitch over a bunker with a 6-iron in your hand, or a 70-yard shot to an elevated green with only a 4-iron to use!

One of the beauties of golf is that the nature of the game lends itself to such a wide variety of competitive contests other than standard stroke play. If you happen to frown on such games as not being "real golf," I urge you to suspend that attitude for a little while and give one or two of them a try. As a member of the Senior Tour, I've made it a point to try to introduce a few of them to my pro-am playing partners in every tournament I play in, in hopes that it will make golf more enjoyable for them. That, truly, is the point of playing.

—Tommy Aaron

INTRODUCTION

Golf is one of the most popular leisure activities in the world today. This growth trend is sure to continue as golfers introduce their friends to this healthy and challenging outdoor sport.

While the classic game of golf, officially called "stroke play" or "medal play," is by far the most popular version, golf is not limited to a single format. There are many different games and competitions that can be played on a golf course. Some are games that emphasize a particular skill, such as putting or driving; others are games of scoring strategy; and still others introduce an element of chance. A golfer may compete against par, or against other golfers. Games can be played by a single player, by a pair or foursome, or even in a tournament with 100 or more participants.

The Games of Golf was written to help the average golfer understand how forty-nine different golf competitions are played and scored. Included are the basic rules for each game, plus strategies to help the player perform as well as possible in the various events.

The book is divided into four sections. Each section includes games for each of the four basic types of games: stroke play, match play, point play, and single shot events/other competitions. Here's a brief summary of each:

Stroke (or Medal) Play is the basic game of golf: a player's score is the total number of strokes he takes to complete the round. The player with the fewest strokes wins. Players can compete against par, or against each other. The games can be scored by the actual number of strokes (called gross score) or by the actual score minus the player's handicap (called net score). Stroke Play is one of the most challenging types of game for the player, since every stroke counts.

Match Play involves head-to-head competition between players. It is played by holes instead of by total score: the winner of the match is the player who takes the most holes during the round.

In Match Play the player who holes out in fewer strokes than his opponent wins that hole. Obviously, when one player is ahead by more holes than there are left to play, the match is over. Because holes are counted, rather than the actual number of strokes in a round, it is possible for a player to take several more strokes during the round than his opponent and still win by taking more holes.

Point Tournaments are played like Stroke Play events, but a set number of points are awarded for eagles, birdies, pars and bogies. Thus, instead of coming up with a score comprised of the actual number of strokes you have taken, a player will have a point total relative to how many holes he scored well enough on to gain points.

When a player in a Point Tournament has gone higher than a bogey he cannot score any points, and at that point he should pick up his ball in the interest of speeding up play. This type of game is efficient when dealing with a large number of players, or when there are time constraints that must be considered to accommodate the needs of your group.

Single Shot Play/Other Events includes events that can be added into any type of tournament, or indeed to any golf outing, to add to the fun and enjoyment of those participating. Also included in this section are special tournaments that require an open golf course and should be planned only when the course will be uncrowded.

As you peruse *The Games of Golf,* you will notice sample scorecards for many of the games. These scorecards show the easiest method of scoring each type of event. The best way for you to learn a game is to read the brief explanation provided, then study the sample scorecard. Once you have learned the game yourself, you can look at your own scorecard at any time during the round to see where you and your partners (or opponents) stand in the competition.

It is my hope that *The Games of Golf* will help you to enjoy the many different kinds of golf competitions. All of these games can be played by golfers of every skill level, from beginner to champion. Indeed, some of them are designed so that golfers with different skill levels can compete together. Playing a variety of games is fun, and I hope your game will improve as you enjoy them.

—David Rihm

THE GAMES
OF GOLF

PART I STROKE OR MEDAL PLAY

INDIVIDUAL STROKE PLAY

Stroke or Medal Play is one of the most widely played golfing events in the world. It is the format used for almost all professional events, and it is appropriate for any number of competitors, from two on up. This form of play is the basic game of golf: a player's score is the total number of strokes he takes to complete the round. The player with the fewest strokes wins.

While this is one of the most challenging games for the player, it is the easiest game for the scorekeeper, who simply

HOLE		1	2	3	4	5	6	7	8	9	OUT
BLUE COURSE RATING 73.5		372	216	413	525	357	436	568	182	396	3465
WHITE COURSE RATING 70.0		349	165	350	492	348	395	517	160	353	3129
HANDICAP		7	13	3	9	17	5	1	15	11	
PAR		4	3	4	5	4	4	5	3	4	36
PETER	5	4	3	4	6	3	4	5	4	4	37
+/–											
JOHN	17	6	4	5	5	7	5	5	3	5	45
PAR		4	3	4	5	4	4	5	3	4	36
HANDICAP		7	15	3	11	17	5	1	13	9	
RED COURSE RATING 71.0		331	100	310	462	304	355	484	110	310	2766
DATE:	SCORER:										

In straight Stroke Play a player's actual score is recorded for each hole. Each nine-hole side is totaled and added together to get the player's 18-hole score. Then his handicap may

records each player's number of strokes. The card is totaled for each nine holes, and for the full eighteen.

Most club tournaments, and often foursomes, recognize both the low gross (actual score) and the low net (actual score minus the player's handicap). Under the net (or handicap) format of scoring all levels of players have an equal chance to win.

If a competition is longer than one day, the total of the scores of each day's play are added together. The winner is the player with the lowest combined total.

10	11	12	13	14	15	16	17	18	IN	TOT	HCP	NET
515	197	380	390	429	230	481	501	448	3571	7036		
475	163	351	350	382	197	426	465	428	3237	6366		
6	18	14	8	16	4	2	10	12				
5	3	4	4	4	3	4	5	4	36	72		
5	4	5	4	4	4	5	5	5	41	78	5	73
5	4	5	5	4	3	5	6	6	43	88	17	71
5	3	4	4	4	3	5	5	5	38	74		
6	18	4	10	16	2	12	8	14				
420	141	333	299	346	166	398	434	398	2935	5701		

ATTEST:
CHECK TEES PLAYED: ☐ BLUE   ☐ WHITE   ☐ RED

be deducted to get his net score.

FOUR BALL
BEST BALL STROKE

Sometimes known as Better Ball of Partners, this variation of the basic stroke play event is a very popular format for many club tournaments around the world. In this game two players team up as partners; on each hole, the better score of the two partners counts as the team's score for that hole. Each player plays the course as if they were playing an individual round, but only the better ball of the two players is recorded. Thus, at the end of the round their team produces a score which would be similar to a score for one player.

This game can be scored either gross, net, or both for the team total. It is a flexible and fun game, because even if you have a poor day, your partner may play well and carry the team. If you help out on a few holes, at the end of the day your team may end up with a very good score.

In this event it is important to be conscious of how your partner stands in the selection of your shots. If he is in good position your strategy and shot selection may be quite different from the strategy you would use if he has gotten into trouble.

HOLE		1	2	3	4	5	6	7	8	9	OUT
BLUE COURSE RATING 73.5		372	216	413	525	357	436	568	182	396	3465
WHITE COURSE RATING 70.0		349	165	350	492	348	395	517	160	353	3129
HANDICAP		7	13	3	9	17	5	1	15	11	
PAR		4	3	4	5	4	4	5	3	4	36
BRIAN	14	5'	4'	4'	6'	4	4'	5'	3	6'	41
FRANK	22	6'	4'	6"	8'	4'	5'	5"	5'	6'	49
+/-											
B.B. GROSS		5	4	4	6	4	4	5	3	6	41
B.B. NET		4	3	3	5	3	3	3	3	5	32
PAR		4	3	4	5	4	4	5	3	4	36
HANDICAP		7	15	3	11	17	5	1	13	9	
RED COURSE RATING 71.0		331	100	310	462	304	355	484	110	310	2766
DATE:	SCORER:										

To make scoring easier on yourself keep track of your team's best ball on each hole as you play. Best ball gross is the lowest actual score of the partners, and best ball net is the lowest

Four Ball Best Ball Stroke play also differs from a regular individual event because, in the interest of speeding up play, you can pick up your ball once it is obvious you cannot produce a lower score than your partner on a given hole. This helps to move large tournaments around the course in a reasonable amount of time, making the game much more enjoyable for all.

In the example, Brian is a 14 handicap and the 14 holes on which he receives a stroke are so designated by slashes on his scoring grid. Frank, a 21 handicap, receives a stroke on every hole, plus an additional stroke on the three toughest holes (designated as 1, 2, and 3 on the handicap row of the scorecard). Two slash marks identify the holes where Frank receives two handicap strokes.

As you can see, Brian played a fairly consistent game and his ball counted most of the time. Frank, on the other hand, did not play up to his handicap, but did have a few very good holes where he helped produce a very good team score, particularly with the net score.

10	11	12	13	14	15	16	17	18	IN	TOT	HCP	NET
515	197	380	390	429	230	481	501	448	3571	7036		
475	163	351	350	382	197	426	465	428	3237	6366		
6	18	14	8	16	4	2	10	12				
5	3	4	4	4	3	4	5	4	36	72		
6'	3	5'	4'	4	4'	5'	5'	6'	42	83	14	69
4'	5'	6'	6'	4'	5'	5"	6'	5'	46	95	21	74
4	3	5	4	4	4	5	5	5	39	80		
3	3	4	3	3	3	3	4	4	30	62		
5	3	4	4	4	3	5	5	5	38	74		
6	18	4	10	16	2	12	8	14				
420	141	333	299	346	166	398	434	398	2935	5701		

ATTEST:
CHECK TEES PLAYED: ☐ BLUE   ☐ WHITE   ☐ RED

score of the partners minus any handicap strokes that they are allocated on that hole.

BEST BALL
OF FOURSOME

In this event each foursome counts only the best score on each hole within their group to make their team's score. This is one of the most popular formats for weekend tournament play on the club level. Because only the best scores for each hole count, a foursome can end up with a very low total for the round.

A Best Ball of Foursome event can be scored in several ways, and it's best to choose the method that fits the ability levels of all the players involved. For instance, if you have a small field with a wide variety of players a "net only" format will keep the competition keen. If the field is larger, with a good mixture of all ability levels, it's advisable to score both gross and net, with winners determined for both categories. On occasions when all the

HOLE		1	2	3	4	5	6	7	8	9	OUT
BLUE COURSE RATING 73.5		372	216	413	525	357	436	568	182	396	3465
WHITE COURSE RATING 70.0		349	165	350	492	348	395	517	160	353	3129
HANDICAP		7	13	3	9	17	5	1	15	11	
PAR		4	3	4	5	4	4	5	3	4	36
PAUL	8	4'	4	4'	6	4	4'	4'	4	5	
PETER	12	5'	3	5'	5'	4	5'	6'	3	5'	
+/- JOHN	10	6'	4	4'	4'	5	5'	5'	3	4	
RICK	18	5'	4'	6'	6'	4'	5'	7'	4'	4'	
NET B.B.		3	3	3	3	3	3	3	3	3	27
PAR		4	3	4	5	4	4	5	3	4	36
HANDICAP		7	15	3	11	17	5	1	13	9	
RED COURSE RATING 71.0		331	100	310	462	304	355	484	110	310	2766
DATE:		SCORER:									

The best net score registered on each hole makes up the team's score in this event.

players are accomplished golfers, a straight gross event is appropriate.

Very aggressive shot selection by all members of the foursome is the key to success in this event. It's important, though, for you to be aware of how your fellow foursome members stand, and what shots everyone in the foursome is facing. If a couple of partners have gotten into trouble or are facing difficult shots, playing percentage shots should be your call. That way you can assure that the team as a whole will avoid a bad score on the hole.

Best Ball of Foursome events take the pressure off individuals to perform well on every shot. If a player has a bad hole or two he can still come back with a good one and contribute to the team's effort.

	10	11	12	13	14	15	16	17	18	IN	TOT	HCP	NET
	515	197	380	390	429	230	481	501	448	3571	7036		
	475	163	351	350	382	197	426	465	428	3237	6366		
	6	18	14	8	16	4	2	10	12				
	5	3	4	4	4	3	4	5	4	36	72		
	6'	3	5	5'	4	3'	5'	5	5				
	5'	5	5	4'	6	3'	5'	6'	5'				
	7'	3	5	4'	5	4'	4'	5'	5				
	8'	4'	5'	6'	5'	4'	5'	7'	4'				
	4	3	4	3	4	2	3	4	3	30	57		
	5	3	4	4	4	3	5	5	5	38	74		
	6	18	4	10	16	2	12	8	14				
	420	141	333	299	346	166	398	434	398	2935	5701		

ATTEST:
CHECK TEES PLAYED: ☐ BLUE   ☐ WHITE   ☐ RED

TWO BEST BALLS OF FOURSOME

In this event the team is a foursome. The two low or best balls of the foursome are added together to make the team's score on each hole. Two Best Balls of the Foursome is a popular format for pro-am games and weekend tournaments since you need at least two players scoring well on every hole. Thus the challenge for the team is greater than a Best Ball of the

Two Best Balls of Foursome: "one gross, one net" rules

HOLE		1	2	3	4	5	6	7	8	9	OUT	
BLUE COURSE RATING 73.5		372	216	413	525	357	436	568	182	396	3465	
WHITE COURSE RATING 70.0		349	165	350	492	348	395	517	160	353	3129	
HANDICAP		7	13	3	9	17	5	1	15	11		
PAR		4	3	4	5	4	4	5	3	4	36	
JOHN	10	4'	3	5'	6'	4	5'	6'	3	5		
JACK	12	5'	3	6'	6'	5	4'	6'	3	4'		
+/- BOB	20	6'	4'	7'	6'	5'	5'	6"	5'	5'		
TOM	18	5'	5'	5'	7'	4'	6'	7'	3'	4'		
2 B.B. (1 GROSS, 1 NET)		8	6	9	11	7	8	10	5	7	71	
PAR		4	3	4	5	4	4	5	3	4	36	
HANDICAP		7	15	3	11	17	5	1	13	9		
RED COURSE RATING 71.0		331	100	310	462	304	355	484	110	310	2766	
DATE:	SCORER:											

The low gross score and the low net score on each hole are totaled on each hole to form the team's score in this event. Note that a player's score can only be counted as either the

Foursome event, where only one ball counts and a team could win by riding a player with a hot hand for that day.

There are two ways of scoring Two Best Balls of Foursome to derive a team total. One way is to use the two low net balls on each hole. The other is to add one gross score and one net score to make the team's score on each hole.

	10	11	12	13	14	15	16	17	18	IN	TOT	HCP	NET
	515	197	380	390	429	230	481	501	448	3571	7036		
	475	163	351	350	382	197	426	465	428	3237	6366		
	6	18	14	8	16	4	2	10	12				
	5	3	4	4	4	3	4	5	4	36	72		
	4'	3	5	4'	4	4'	5'	7'	4				
	5'	4	5	5'	4	4'	6'	5'	7'				
	6'	5'	7'	5'	6'	3'	5"	6'	6'				
	6'	5'	6'	4'	5'	4'	5'	7'	6'				
	8	7	10	7	8	6	8	10	9	73	144		
	5	3	4	4	4	3	5	5	5	38	74		
	6	18	4	10	16	2	12	8	14				
	420	141	333	299	346	166	398	434	398	2935	5701		

ATTEST:
CHECK TEES PLAYED: ☐ BLUE ☐ WHITE ☐ RED

gross or the net score, but not as both.

No matter which format you choose, each player must be aware of how his partners stand at all times. This is so that unnecessary risks are not taken that could ruin the score of the team. On the other hand, if a couple of team members are sitting in good shape, a player is free to attempt a very risky shot that he might never try under normal circumstances. This gives the game an exciting team-play aspect: a risky shot might be the right choice since you have everything to gain

Two Best Balls of Foursome: "two net" rules

HOLE		1	2	3	4	5	6	7	8	9	OUT
BLUE COURSE RATING 73.5		372	216	413	525	357	436	568	182	396	3465
WHITE COURSE RATING 70.0		349	165	350	492	348	395	517	160	353	3129
HANDICAP		7	13	3	9	17	5	1	15	11	
PAR		4	3	4	5	4	4	5	3	4	36
JOHN	10	4'	3	5'	6'	4	5'	6'	3	5	
JACK	12	5'	3	6'	6'	5	4'	6'	3	4'	
+/- BOB	20	6'	4'	7'	6'	5'	5'	6"	5'	5'	
TOM	18	5'	5'	5'	7'	4'	6'	7'	3'	4'	
2 B.B.NET		7	6	8	10	7	7	9	5	6	65
PAR		4	3	4	5	4	4	5	3	4	36
HANDICAP		7	15	3	11	17	5	1	13	9	
RED COURSE RATING 71.0		331	100	310	462	304	355	484	110	310	2766
DATE:	SCORER:										

Adding the two low net scores on each hole of the foursome together makes up the team's score in this event. Consistent play and staying par or better on every hole is difficult, but

and nothing to lose.

Team events such as these are popular because individual golf is a difficult game for the average player to score well in consistently. Team play allows players to have some bad holes without jeopardizing their chances of winning the event providing the team members play well at the right times. Study the following examples of both formats so that you understand the method of scoring for each.

	10	11	12	13	14	15	16	17	18	IN	TOT	HCP	NET
	515	197	380	390	429	230	481	501	448	3571	7036		
	475	163	351	350	382	197	426	465	428	3237	6366		
	6	18	14	8	16	4	2	10	12				
	5	3	4	4	4	3	4	5	4	36	72		
	4'	3	5	4'	4	4'	5'	7'	4				
	5'	4	5	5'	4	4'	6'	5'	7'				
	6'	5'	7'	5'	6	3'	5"	6'	6'				
	6'	5'	6'	4'	5'	4'	5'	7'	6'				
	7	7	10	6	8	5	7	9	9	68	133		
	5	3	4	4	4	3	5	5	5	38	74		
	6	18	4	10	16	2	12	8	14				
	420	141	333	299	346	166	398	434	398	2935	5701		

ATTEST:
CHECK TEES PLAYED: ☐ BLUE ☐ WHITE ☐ RED

if you can do it, you will be near the top of the leader board when all the scores are turned in.

FOUR BALL AGGREGATE

This is a partners event in which both players' scores are recorded. While this is a tough event on the players because every shot counts, it does reward the team that had the two best players on that given day. In other events, such as Four Ball Best Ball, a team can win with only one good player. In Four Ball Aggregate the winning team is the one with the best combination of players on the field that day.

Most often this event is played on a handicap basis. To score it, simply total each partner's net score on each hole, then total those scores at the end of the round. The team with the lowest combined net score when all groups have returned their scores is the winner.

In this sort of tournament, where each player's score counts, it is very important to play a consistent game. Knowing your game and the odds of executing certain types of shots, therefore, are crucial

HOLE	1	2	3	4	5	6	7	8	9	OUT
BLUE COURSE RATING 73.5	372	216	413	525	357	436	568	182	396	3465
WHITE COURSE RATING 70.0	349	165	350	492	348	395	517	160	353	3129
HANDICAP	7	13	3	9	17	5	1	15	11	
PAR	4	3	4	5	4	4	5	3	4	36
JOE 10	5'	3	5'	5'	5	4'	6'	3	5	41
BOB 21	5'	4'	6"	6'	4'	5'	6"	3'	6'	45
+/- AGGREGATE	8	6	8	9	8	7	9	5	10	70
PAR	4	3	4	5	4	4	5	3	4	36
HANDICAP	7	15	3	11	17	5	1	13	9	
RED COURSE RATING 71.0	331	100	310	462	304	355	484	110	310	2766
DATE:	SCORER:									

In the example above each player's net score (actual score minus applicable handicap strokes)

to success. More often than not, playing a safer shot that may cost you one stroke will in the long run save more strokes. If you attempt a very difficult shot and it does not end up the way you had hoped, you may waste many strokes trying to recover. Study your shot selection carefully and stick to your game plan. Players should only attempt shots that they are likely to make, and that will keep them out of trouble if a shot goes awry.

In the example, Joe and Bob keep their scores as they normally would. In the row below their names is the aggregate of their net scores for each hole. Handicap strokes are marked with a slash mark. [Since Bob is a 21 handicap he receives two strokes on the three most difficult holes on the course.] To be sure no scoring errors have been made along the way, each player's total net score should be combined and checked against the hole-by-hole total at the end of the round.

	10	11	12	13	14	15	16	17	18	IN	TOT	HCP	NET
	515	197	380	390	429	230	481	501	448	3571	7036		
	475	163	351	350	382	197	426	465	428	3237	6366		
	6	18	14	8	16	4	2	10	12				
	5	3	4	4	4	3	4	5	4	36	72		
	5'	4'	5	4'5	4'	5'	5'	5		42	83	10	73
	6'	3'	7'	5'5'	4'5"	7'	5'			47	92	21	71
	9	6	11	7	9	6	7	10	9	74	144		144
	5	3	4	4	4	3	5	5	5	38	74		
	6	18	4	10	16	2	12	8	14				
	420	141	333	299	346	166	398	434	398	2935	5701		

ATTEST:
CHECK TEES PLAYED: ☐ BLUE   ☐ WHITE   ☐ RED

is added together to get the team's aggregate on each hole.

ALTERNATE SHOT (FOURSOMES)

Alternate Shot is a stroke play event played with a partner, but using only one ball for the team. Both players drive off the first tee and select the drive in the best position. From that point on they alternate shots with their partner for the rest of the round. If player A's tee shot is chosen on the first hole, for instance, player B will hit player A's ball as the team's second shot. Player A then hits the third shot, and so on. If player A holes out, then on the next hole player B hits the tee shot.

This event is scored just like an Individual Stroke Play event. Only the gross score needs to be kept during the round. At

HOLE	1	2	3	4	5	6	7	8	9	OUT	
BLUE COURSE RATING 73.5	372	216	413	525	357	436	568	182	396	3465	
WHITE COURSE RATING 70.0	349	165	350	492	348	395	517	160	353	3129	
HANDICAP	7	13	3	9	17	5	1	15	11		
PAR	4	3	4	5	4	4	5	3	4	36	
BILL SMITH 12	5	4	6	6	5	4	7	4	5	46	
JUDY SMITH 32											
+/-											
PAR	4	3	4	5	4	4	5	3	4	36	
HANDICAP	7	15	3	11	17	5	1	13	9		
RED COURSE RATING 71.0	331	100	310	462	304	355	484	110	310	2766	
DATE:	SCORER:										

In Alternate Shot the team's actual score is recorded on each hole. When you have completed 18 holes one-half of the team's combined handicap is deducted from the gross score to get

the end of the round the team's net score is obtained by taking one half of the combined total of the two players' handicaps and deducting it from their gross score.

If either player incurs a penalty stroke, it does not change the rotation of play. This also includes the playing of a provisional ball should you suspect a ball may be lost or out of bounds.

Alternate Shot is a popular format at many clubs, particularly in their mixed championships. Naturally, the ladies play off their own tees when it is their turn to tee off on a particular hole.

	10	11	12	13	14	15	16	17	18	IN	TOT	HCP	NET
	515	197	380	390	429	230	481	501	448	3571	7036		
	475	163	351	350	382	197	426	465	428	3237	6366		
	6	18	14	8	16	4	2	10	12				
	5	3	4	4	4	3	4	5	4	36	72		
	5	4	5	4	6	4	4	6	5	43	89	22	67
	5	3	4	4	4	3	5	5	5	38	74		
	6	18	4	10	16	2	12	8	14				
	420	141	333	299	346	166	398	434	398	2935	5701		

ATTEST:
CHECK TEES PLAYED: ☐ BLUE   ☐ WHITE   ☐ RED

the team's net score.

PINEHURST FOURSOMES

In this variation of Alternate Shot (Foursomes) each player tees off on every hole. The tee shot considered to be in the best position is chosen and the other ball is picked up. Play from this point on is alternate shot until the ball is holed out.

This variation of Alternate Shot (Foursomes) is a little easier on the teams since they have two tee shots to choose from on every hole. It gives the players options that they would not have in the other format. For instance, if the first player's tee shot is in good position, the second player can really go after

HOLE		1	2	3	4	5	6	7	8	9	OUT
BLUE COURSE RATING 73.5		372	216	413	525	357	436	568	182	396	3465
WHITE COURSE RATING 70.0		349	165	350	492	348	395	517	160	353	3129
HANDICAP		7	13	3	9	17	5	1	15	11	
PAR		4	3	4	5	4	4	5	3	4	36
JOE	17	4	4	5	5	5	4	6	4	4	41
HAROLD	11										
+/−											
PAR		4	3	4	5	4	4	5	3	4	36
HANDICAP		7	15	3	11	17	5	1	13	9	
RED COURSE RATING 71.0		331	100	310	462	304	355	484	110	310	2766
DATE:		SCORER:									

This event is scored just like an Alternate Shot event. The team's actual score is entered on each hole with the applicable team handicap deducted from the gross total at the end of

his shot knowing that if the shot ends up in trouble the other ball is in a playable position. On the other hand, if the first player's shot ends up in trouble the second player can change his strategy and play a high percentage shot to be sure that the team has a ball in a playable position for the next shot.

Scoring is the same as in the Alternate Shot (Foursomes) format. The team has one score for each hole. If a net format is chosen 50 percent of the two players' combined handicap is deducted from their gross score at the end of the round.

	10	11	12	13	14	15	16	17	18	IN	TOT	HCP	NET
	515	197	380	390	429	230	481	501	448	3571	7036		
	475	163	351	350	382	197	426	465	428	3237	6366		
	6	18	14	8	16	4	2	10	12				
	5	3	4	4	4	3	4	5	4	36	72		
	6	4	4	5	4	4	5	6	4	42	83	14	69
	5	3	4	4	4	3	5	5	5	38	74		
	6	18	4	10	16	2	12	8	14				
	420	141	333	299	346	166	398	434	398	2935	5701		

ATTEST:
CHECK TEES PLAYED: ☐ BLUE   ☐ WHITE   ☐ RED

the round.

CHAPMAN FOURSOMES

This is a variation of the Alternate Shot tournament where both players hit two shots on every hole and then the ball in the best position after two shots is played out in the alternate shot format until the hole is completed. On each hole both players tee off, then they switch balls to play their second shots (player A hits B's drive for his second shot and vice versa). After both players have hit two shots, the ball that is in the best position is chosen and you play alternate shot until the hole is completed (on par three holes only, each player hits a tee shot; then the best-positioned ball is chosen and from that point on the partners alternate shots until holing out).

HOLE	1	2	3	4	5	6	7	8	9	OUT
BLUE COURSE RATING 73.5	372	216	413	525	357	436	568	182	396	3465
WHITE COURSE RATING 70.0	349	165	350	492	348	395	517	160	353	3129
HANDICAP	7	13	3	9	17	5	1	15	11	
PAR	4	3	4	5	4	4	5	3	4	36
GEORGE 12	5	4	5	7	5	5	6	3	5	45
BRIDGET 36										
+/–										
PAR	4	3	4	5	4	4	5	3	4	36
HANDICAP	7	15	3	11	17	5	1	13	9	
RED COURSE RATING 71.0	331	100	310	462	304	355	484	110	310	2766
DATE:	SCORER:									

In a Chapman Foursomes event scores are usually the lowest of the three alternate shot formats because each player will hit two shots on each hole (except on par threes), thereby giving

Again, scoring is just like an Individual Stroke Play event where the team ends up with one score for each hole. At the end of the round the team deducts one-half of their combined handicap from their gross score to produce a net score.

This format allows you to play more shots in the round than you would hit in a true alternate shot format. It's also easier for you to score well in, since on every hole you and your partner are playing two balls for two shots before beginning to alternate. This means you have a chance for a good score on a hole even if one ball goes out of play.

	10	11	12	13	14	15	16	17	18	IN	TOT	HCP	NET
	515	197	380	390	429	230	481	501	448	3571	7036		
	475	163	351	350	382	197	426	465	428	3237	6366		
	6	18	14	8	16	4	2	10	12				
	5	3	4	4	4	3	4	5	4	36	72		
	5	4	5	6	4	3	5	6	5	43	88	24	64
	5	3	4	4	4	3	5	5	5	38	74		
	6	18	4	10	16	2	12	8	14				
	420	141	333	299	346	166	398	434	398	2935	5701		

ATTEST:
CHECK TEES PLAYED: ☐ BLUE ☐ WHITE ☐ RED

the team a better chance to pick good shots.

THROW OUT
WORST HOLES

In this event each competitor is allowed to throw out a certain number of his worst holes. The number of holes to be thrown out at the end of the round is determined before play starts. Generally, it is best to throw out no more than three holes because if more than that are thrown out the scores can become distorted.

The Throw Out Worst Holes event should be played as a stroke play event. At the completion of the round each player will subtract the number of his worst holes from the gross total that he is allowed under the rules set forth for that day (in our example it is the two worst holes). From the new gross total the players' handicaps are subtracted and the net scores are

HOLE		1	2	3	4	5	6	7	8	9	OUT
BLUE COURSE RATING 73.5		372	216	413	525	357	436	568	182	396	3465
WHITE COURSE RATING 70.0		349	165	350	492	348	395	517	160	353	3129
HANDICAP		7	13	3	9	17	5	1	15	11	
PAR		4	3	4	5	4	4	5	3	4	36
JACK	*10*	*5*	*4*	*4*	*4*	*5*	*5*	*7*	*4*	*6*	*44*
								7		*6*	*31*
+/-											
HAROLD	*17*	*5*	*4*	*5*	*6*	*6*	*5*	*5*	*5*	*5*	*46*
						6					*40*
PAR		4	3	4	5	4	4	5	3	4	36
HANDICAP		7	15	3	11	17	5	1	13	9	
RED COURSE RATING 71.0		331	100	310	462	304	355	484	110	310	2766
DATE:	SCORER:										

In a Throw Out Worst Holes event deduct the highest numbers that you can. In our example, the two worst holes are deducted from the players' gross scores and then their handicap is compared, with the lowest total being the winner of the event.

This is a good format to use in early-season play when golfers are still a little rusty from the long winter layoff. By allowing each player to take out a few of his worst holes, it gives even the player who finds a lot of trouble a better chance of winning. Players should try to play a little more aggressively since there will not be so much of a penalty if risky shots do not turn out well. Obviously, too, once you have had a couple of bad holes you should become a little more conservative—you don't want to use up all of your throw-out holes right at the beginning!

10	11	12	13	14	15	16	17	18	IN	TOT	HCP	NET
515	197	380	390	429	230	481	501	448	3571	7036		
475	163	351	350	382	197	426	465	428	3237	6366		
6	18	14	8	16	4	2	10	12				
5	3	4	4	4	3	4	5	4	36	72		
5	3	5	5	4	3	5	5	5	40	84		
									40	71	10	61
6	5	5	5	6	4	7	5	6	49	95		
							7		42	82	17	65
5	3	4	4	4	3	5	5	5	38	74		
6	18	4	10	16	2	12	8	14				
420	141	333	299	346	166	398	434	398	2935	5701		

ATTEST:
CHECK TEES PLAYED: ☐ BLUE ☐ WHITE ☐ RED

deducted from that new total to produce their net scores.

CRIERS' COMPETITION

The Criers' Competition is a stroke play event where each player is allowed to pick a predetermined number of his worst holes and revert his score on them back to par. Any number of holes can be decided upon, but it is most common to pick just two or three holes. Winners should be chosen for both low gross and low net scores.

This is a good event to use when there is a group of golfers who do not play much and tend to have a few very bad holes. By changing two or three of each player's scores back to par all of the scores will end up closer together. Also, the players will still have a chance of winning this event even though they might have a couple of disastrous holes which would almost immediately knock them out of contention in a normal stroke play event.

In the example, George and Peter have just completed a Criers'

HOLE		1	2	3	4	5	6	7	8	9	OUT
BLUE COURSE RATING 73.5		372	216	413	525	357	436	568	182	396	3465
WHITE COURSE RATING 70.0		349	165	350	492	348	395	517	160	353	3129
HANDICAP		7	13	3	9	17	5	1	15	11	
PAR		4	3	4	5	4	4	5	3	4	36
GEORGE	15	4	4	5	6	⑦ 4	4	5	4	5	44 41
+/-											
PETER	10	5	3	4	6	5	⑧ 4	5	3	5	44 40
PAR		4	3	4	5	4	4	5	3	4	36
HANDICAP		7	15	3	11	17	5	1	13	9	
RED COURSE RATING 71.0		331	100	310	462	304	355	484	110	310	2766
DATE:	SCORER:										

In a Criers' Competition you are allowed to change back to par your score on a predetermined number of holes. Choose the holes that are the most over par, not just the highest numbers

Tournament where each player is allowed to change two of his worst holes back to par. If you look at George's score carefully you will note that he made two 7's and two 6's. He chose to change one of the 6's and one of the 7's because they were both three over par for those particular holes. He did not choose the other 7 because it was only two over par, thus it would have reduced his score by only two shots on that hole and not by three shots like the six did on the par three hole. Peter's score on the other hand is very straightforward: the two holes he reverted back to par are the two highest numbers on his card. You can see, then, that it is important to look over your scorecard very carefully, checking for each hole the total number of strokes over par, rather than the total number of strokes per se. That way you will reduce your score by the maximum number of strokes possible.

	10	11	12	13	14	15	16	17	18	IN	TOT	HCP	NET
	515	197	380	390	429	230	481	501	448	3571	7036		
	475	163	351	350	382	197	426	465	428	3237	6366		
	6	18	14	8	16	4	2	10	12				
	5	3	4	4	4	3	4	5	4	36	72		
	7	3	5	5	4	(6)	5	5	5	45	89		
					3					42	83	15	68
	4	3	5	(7)	5	4	4	5	4	41	85		
				4						38	78	10	68
	5	3	4	4	4	3	5	5	5	38	74		
	6	18	4	10	16	2	12	8	14				
	420	141	333	299	346	166	398	434	398	2935	5701		

ATTEST:
CHECK TEES PLAYED: ☐ BLUE   ☐ WHITE   ☐ RED

on your card.

SELECTED
SCORE

This is a two-round, 36-hole event. Each contestant selects his best score on each hole from the two rounds that he played. The player with the lowest score for his 18 best holes is the winner. This can be played as either a gross or net event (when using net score, players should deduct only 75 percent of their handicap from their 18-hole score).

In this event some very aggressive play is needed to finish well. In the first round it may be wise to be a little cautious and get in a solid score. In the second round you know where your first-round good and bad holes were, so you can

HOLE			1	2	3	4	5	6	7	8	9	OUT
BLUE COURSE RATING 73.5			372	216	413	525	357	436	568	182	396	3465
WHITE COURSE RATING 70.0			349	165	350	492	348	395	517	160	353	3129
HANDICAP			7	13	3	9	17	5	1	15	11	
PAR			4	3	4	5	4	4	5	3	4	36
BILL	*1ST.*		4	3	4	5	4	6	6	3	5	
	2ND.		4	2	5	6	4	4	6	4	5	
+/-												
SELECTED			4	2	4	5	4	4	6	3	5	37
PAR			4	3	4	5	4	4	5	3	4	36
HANDICAP			7	15	3	11	17	5	1	13	9	
RED COURSE RATING 71.0			331	100	310	462	304	355	484	110	310	2766
DATE:		SCORER:										

The player keeps his score for two rounds on one card in a Selected Score event with the best score on each hole counting as his final total. The total of Bill's best holes for the two

play conservatively on the holes that you scored poorly on in the first round, and aggressively on the holes that were your best.

This is a good early-season event because a number of poor holes in a round will not put a player out of the tournament. A player could have a poor first round and play well the second round, and thus improve his score by a large number of strokes. On the other hand, a good first round may make the second round somewhat frustrating because the player may not be able to improve on any of the first-round scores.

10	11	12	13	14	15	16	17	18	IN	TOT	HCP	NET
515	197	380	390	429	230	481	501	448	3571	7036		
475	163	351	350	382	197	426	465	428	3237	6366		
6	18	14	8	16	4	2	10	12				
5	3	4	4	4	3	4	5	4	36	72		
5	2	4	3	5	3	5	6	4				
5	3	4	4	4	4	5	5	4				
5	2	4	3	4	3	5	5	4	35	72		
5	3	4	4	4	3	5	5	5	38	74		
6	18	4	10	16	2	12	8	14				
420	141	333	299	346	166	398	434	398	2935	5701		

ATTEST:
CHECK TEES PLAYED: ☐ BLUE ☐ WHITE ☐ RED

rounds comes out to an even par 72.

RINGER COMPETITION

This competition is a stroke play event and is extended over the whole season. The exact length of the tournament must be decided before the start of the event so that all players know how long they have to complete all of their rounds.

The Ringer score is the lowest score the player achieves on each hole during the length of the event. At the end of the event these scores are totaled and the player with the lowest total is the winner. The Ringer Competition can be scored on both a gross and net basis (however, in net scoring only one-

HOLE	1	2	3	4	5	6	7	8	9	OUT
BLUE COURSE RATING 73.5	372	216	413	525	357	436	568	182	396	3465
WHITE COURSE RATING 70.0	349	165	350	492	348	395	517	160	353	3129
HANDICAP	7	13	3	9	17	5	1	15	11	
PAR	4	3	4	5	4	4	5	3	4	36
JOHN JOHNSON 9	3	2	3	3	4	3	4	2	3	27
+/-										
PAR	4	3	4	5	4	4	5	3	4	36
HANDICAP	7	15	3	11	17	5	1	13	9	
RED COURSE RATING 71.0	331	100	310	462	304	355	484	110	310	2766
DATE:	SCORER:									

A player's Ringer scorecard should be adjusted after each round so that the lowest score he

half of the player's handicap—as his handicap stands at the ending date of the tournament—should be used).

In this season-long event, Ringer scores can be used from any round and it is a good idea to keep a separate Ringer Card that can be updated after each round, so that each player knows how he stands at all times.

This is an interesting event to track because very low 18-hole season totals are possible. The Ringer Card represents each player's best effort, so the winner at the end of the season rightly deserves special recognition.

	10	11	12	13	14	15	16	17	18	IN	TOT	HCP	NET
	515	197	380	390	429	230	481	501	448	3571	7036		
	475	163	351	350	382	197	426	465	428	3237	6366		
	6	18	14	8	16	4	2	10	12				
	5	3	4	4	4	3	4	5	4	36	72		
	4	3	3	3	3	3	4	5	4	32	59		
	5	3	4	4	4	3	5	5	5	38	74		
	6	18	4	10	16	2	12	8	14				
	420	141	333	299	346	166	398	434	398	2935	5701		

ATTEST:
CHECK TEES PLAYED: ☐ BLUE ☐ WHITE ☐ RED

has had on each hole is kept up to date.

BLIND HOLES

In this event after all the players are on the course a certain number of holes (usually from one to three) are drawn from a hat. At the end of everyone's round, the score the players took on those holes is deducted from their total and then their handicap is also deducted to produce a low net winner. This is scored just like a Throw Out Worst Holes event only the same holes are used for all players.

In the example card, holes number 5, 12, and 16 are the blind holes that will be deducted from the players' scores this day. In the row below their actual scores, John and Harry have adjusted their totals after finding out what the blind

HOLE	1	2	3	4	5	6	7	8	9	OUT
BLUE COURSE RATING 73.5	372	216	413	525	357	436	568	182	396	3465
WHITE COURSE RATING 70.0	349	165	350	492	348	395	517	160	353	3129
HANDICAP	7	13	3	9	17	5	1	15	11	
PAR	4	3	4	5	4	4	5	3	4	36
JOHN	5	4	5	5	6	4	5	3	5	42
					6					36
+/-										
HARRY	6	4	5	6	5	5	7	4	5	47
					5					42
PAR	4	3	4	5	4	4	5	3	4	36
HANDICAP	7	15	3	11	17	5	1	13	9	
RED COURSE RATING 71.0	331	100	310	462	304	355	484	110	310	2766
DATE:	SCORER:									

In a Blind Holes event the same holes are deducted from all players' scores (in our example holes number 5, 12 and 16 are the holes that have been selected). The player's handicap

holes were by deducting the score they had on the designated holes from their gross score on each of the nines. The nines are then totaled and their handicaps are deducted to obtain John and Harry's net scores.

This is more of a fun type of event than a "championship" tournament because of the luck or chance of getting the holes that will help you the most drawn from the hat. In our example, if this had been a straight net event, John would have had a net 73 and Harry would have had a net 74. However, the blind holes 12 and 16 were two of Harry's worst holes. Thus the draw helped Harry to have a lower net score than John.

	10	11	12	13	14	15	16	17	18	IN	TOT	HCP	NET
	515	197	380	390	429	230	481	501	448	3571	7036		
	475	163	351	350	382	197	426	465	428	3237	6366		
	6	18	14	8	16	4	2	10	12				
	5	3	4	4	4	3	4	5	4	36	72		
	6	3	4	5	4	5	5	6	5	43	85		
		4				5				34	70	12	58
	7	4	6	6	4	5	7	6	5	50	97		
		6					7			37	79	23	56
	5	3	4	4	4	3	5	5	5	38	74		
	6	18	4	10	16	2	12	8	14				
	420	141	333	299	346	166	398	434	398	2935	5701		

ATTEST:
CHECK TEES PLAYED: ☐ BLUE   ☐ WHITE   ☐ RED

is then deducted from that new total.

BLIND
PARTNERS

In Blind Partners the teams are made up by a blind draw of names from a hat. The draw is made after all players are on the course, so no one knows who their partner is until they have completed play. Since you do not know what your partner may be scoring on any particular hole, this format encourages aggressive play at all times so that you can score as low as possible on every hole.

Many different types of scoring can be used for this type of event. Since a wide range of players will usually be involved

HOLE		1	2	3	4	5	6	7	8	9	OUT
BLUE COURSE RATING 73.5		372	216	413	525	357	436	568	182	396	3465
WHITE COURSE RATING 70.0		349	165	350	492	348	395	517	160	353	3129
HANDICAP		7	13	3	9	17	5	1	15	11	
PAR		4	3	4	5	4	4	5	3	4	36
JOHN	12	5'	3	4'	6'	5	5'	6'	3	5'	
DICK	20	6'	3'	6'	7'	5'	6'	6"	5'	5'	
+/-											
NET BEST BALL		4	2	3	5	4	4	4	3	4	33
PAR		4	3	4	5	4	4	5	3	4	36
HANDICAP		7	15	3	11	17	5	1	13	9	
RED COURSE RATING 71.0		331	100	310	462	304	355	484	110	310	2766
DATE:		SCORER:									

In our example John and Dick were put together as partners in a blind draw from all players entered in the event. The event chosen was a Best Ball of Partners and by simply putting their

in this event, net scores should be used so that all players have a fair chance of winning. The most common formats used are Best Ball of Partners, Aggregate, Match Play vs. Par and Quota. Whatever format you choose, the scores are matched up as the players come in from the course and the team with the lowest total wins.

This is a good tournament format to use to get people to know other golfers. Players will look for the person they were paired up with to exchange notes on their rounds and it can be a great way to make new acquaintances.

	10	11	12	13	14	15	16	17	18	IN	TOT	HCP	NET
	515	197	380	390	429	230	481	501	448	3571	7036		
	475	163	351	350	382	197	426	465	428	3237	6366		
	6	18	14	8	16	4	2	10	12				
	5	3	4	4	4	3	4	5	4	36	72		
	5'	3	4'	3'	5'	4'	4'	6'	4'				
	6'	3'	5'	5'	5'	5'	7"	7'	6'				
	4	2	4	2	4	3	3	5	3	30	63		
	5	3	4	4	4	3	5	5	5	38	74		
	6	18	4	10	16	2	12	8	14				
	420	141	333	299	346	166	398	434	398	2935	5701		

ATTEST:
CHECK TEES PLAYED: ☐ BLUE   ☐ WHITE   ☐ RED

two scores on to one card their Best Ball is very easy to come up with.

SCRAMBLE TOURNAMENTS

Sometimes called Captain and Crew, Scramble involves playing only the best shots of the group. There are many different formats, but the basics of this event are as follows:

First, foursomes are chosen so that the total team handicaps come out as close as possible (you can do this by grouping players as A, B, C, D according to their handicaps, then putting one player from each category on each team).

Once the teams are chosen, members of a foursome drive from the tee and the ball in the best position is selected. All members of the team then play their next shots from the position of the selected ball by dropping or placing their balls within a prescribed distance of that ball (use convenient measurements such as the length of a scorecard or one club length). The best second shot is then chosen and the other balls are placed near it for everyone's third stroke. The team continues selecting the best shot until the ball is holed out.

If the chosen ball is in the rough, a bunker, a water hazard, or on the fringe, the designated distance must keep the remaining balls under the same conditions (for example, you cannot use one club length to put the ball in the fairway when the selected ball was in the rough).

When a ball is selected on the green, a marker should be placed on the green one putter head length away from the ball so that the remaining balls can be placed in the exact same location. Once a ball is holed out, of course, the team is finished, so team members must be cautioned not to make tap-in putts until all the players have had an opportunity to make the first putt.

A Scramble is best played as a gross-score event. However, if there is more than a 15-shot difference between team handicaps, you should go to a net format. Each team's handicap should be established by subtracting 10 percent from the combined handicap of the group. [Note: If there is a team with only three players, to equalize things for them each player on the threesome should be allowed to play two shots on six holes on a rotation set before they tee off. To derive their team handicap, take an average of the three players' handicaps on the team and add it to their total, then reduce by 10 percent, as above.]

Scrambles encourage very aggressive play because if you hit a bad shot one of your partners should be able to put his ball in position to play the next shot. This is a great format to use when there are a lot of duffers in the field—even if they hit a lot of bad shots they will get to pick up their ball and move to a better position. It's also a game that can be played rapidly, since players are not wasting a lot of shots trying to get out of trouble.

Here are some variations of the Scramble format:

Straight Scramble

A. All players play from same tees.
B. Each player plays every shot.
C. Record the team score after each hole.
D. Team handicap is deducted at the end of the round.

Straight Scramble—Variable Tees

A. Class A and B players play from blue tees and class C and D players play from white tees (this should prevent a situation where the team is always selecting the best player's drive).
B. Each player plays every shot.
C. Record the team score for each hole.
D. Team handicap is deducted at the end of the round.

Straight Scramble—Four Tee Shot Rule

A. All players play from same tees.
B. Every player's drive must be used at least four times during the course of the round. (This will take some planning. It's a good idea to try to use up everyone's quota as early as possible so that you don't come down to the last few holes and have to use a player's drive to meet the four tee shot rule.)
C. Each player plays every shot.
D. Record the team score for each hole.
E. The team's handicap is deducted at the end of the round.

Drop Out Scramble

A. All players play from the same tees.
B. The player whose ball is selected does not play the second shot. The player whose ball is selected after the second shot does not hit the third shot. Instead, the player who sat out the second shot is now back in the game. Continue this rotation until the ball is holed out.
C. Record the team score for each hole.
D. The team handicap is deducted at the end of the round.

HOLE		1	2	3	4	5	6	7	8	9	OUT
BLUE COURSE RATING 73.5		372	216	413	525	357	436	568	182	396	3465
WHITE COURSE RATING 70.0		349	165	350	492	348	395	517	160	353	3129
HANDICAP		7	13	3	9	17	5	1	15	11	
PAR		4	3	4	5	4	4	5	3	4	36
BILL	6	4'	3	3	5	4	5'	4	2	4	34
LOREN	18				'						
+/–											
BOB	16		'		'			'		'	
DAVE	10			'					'		
PAR		4	3	4	5	4	4	5	3	4	36
HANDICAP		7	15	3	11	17	5	1	13	9	
RED COURSE RATING 71.0		331	100	310	462	304	355	484	110	310	2766
DATE:		SCORER:									

In a Scramble Tournament the foursome's gross score is recorded on each hole. In the example above the four tee shot rule is in effect so the scorekeeper has tracked whose drive was used

Two Man Scramble

A. All players play from the same tees.
B. The ball in the best position after each shot is chosen and the partner moves his ball to that position for the next shot.
C. Record the team score for each hole; the team handicap will be deducted at the end of the round. In a Two Man Scramble the team's handicap should be 30 percent of the two players' combined handicap.

10	11	12	13	14	15	16	17	18	IN	TOT	HCP	NET
515	197	380	390	429	230	481	501	448	3571	7036		
475	163	351	350	382	197	426	465	428	3237	6366		
6	18	14	8	16	4	2	10	12				
5	3	4	4	4	3	4	5	4	36	72		
4	3'	4	3	4	3	4'	5	3	33	67	5	62
/				/		/						
		/					/					
	/		/									
5	3	4	4	4	3	5	5	5	38	74		
6	18	4	10	16	2	12	8	14				
420	141	333	299	346	166	398	434	398	2935	5701		

ATTEST:
CHECK TEES PLAYED: ☐ BLUE ☐ WHITE ☐ RED

on each hole by marking the card with a slash mark in the scoring grid.

KICKERS
TOURNAMENT

In a Kickers Tournament players start by choosing a range of net score (the most common range is 70 to 80). Then each player picks a handicap they think will put their final net score within that chosen range. After all players are on the course, a ''Kickers number'' within the range is chosen by a blind draw. The players whose net scores equal the number drawn are the winners. If no one comes in with the target score, a

HOLE	1	2	3	4	5	6	7	8	9	OUT
BLUE COURSE RATING 73.5	372	216	413	525	357	436	568	182	396	3465
WHITE COURSE RATING 70.0	349	165	350	492	348	395	517	160	353	3129
HANDICAP	7	13	3	9	17	5	1	15	11	
PAR	4	3	4	5	4	4	5	3	4	36
JOHN	5	5	4	6	4	5	6	3	5	43
BILL	4	4	4	5	5	4	6	4	4	40
+/-										
HARRY	6	4	6	6	5	5	5	4	5	46
TOM	4	3	5	7	5	5	5	3	4	41
PAR	4	3	4	5	4	4	5	3	4	36
HANDICAP	7	15	3	11	17	5	1	13	9	
RED COURSE RATING 71.0	331	100	310	462	304	355	484	110	310	2766
DATE:	SCORER:									

In the example above each player has chosen a handicap that they feel will put their net score between 70 and 80. A blind draw is made to determine the winners when all players have

new number is drawn.

This is a good format to use when there is a large number of players in the tournament or group who do not have established handicaps. It also gives players who are not playing up to their handicap a chance to choose a number they are comfortable with. As long as their net score ends up within the specified range they have an opportunity to win.

	10	11	12	13	14	15	16	17	18	IN	TOT	HCP	NET
	515	197	380	390	429	230	481	501	448	3571	7036		
	475	163	351	350	382	197	426	465	428	3237	6366		
	6	18	14	8	16	4	2	10	12				
	5	3	4	4	4	3	4	5	4	36	72		
	6	5	4	3	5	4	5	5	5	42	85	9	76
	5	4	5	5	4	3	5	6	4	41	81	12	69
	6	4	4	6	5	4	5	6	5	45	91	17	74
	6	5	5	4	5	4	5	4	5	43	84	6	78
	5	3	4	4	4	3	5	5	5	38	74		
	6	18	4	10	16	2	12	8	14				
	420	141	333	299	346	166	398	434	398	2935	5701		

ATTEST:
CHECK TEES PLAYED: ☐ BLUE ☐ WHITE ☐ RED

finished. Note that Bill played better than he thought he might and will not be eligible since his net score did not fall in the range.

KICKERS REPLAY

In this variation of Individual Stroke Play each player is allowed to replay a predetermined number of shots at any time during the round. When a shot has been replayed the player must continue with that ball, even if it is in worse position than the first ball. No shot can be replayed more than once. Generally, to ensure that scores will be in line, no more than six shots should be allowed to be replayed during the round.

In this event the players must use their own judgment in selecting the shots that they want to replay. It is

HOLE	1	2	3	4	5	6	7	8	9	OUT
BLUE COURSE RATING 73.5	372	216	413	525	357	436	568	182	396	3465
WHITE COURSE RATING 70.0	349	165	350	492	348	395	517	160	353	3129
HANDICAP	7	13	3	9	17	5	1	15	11	
PAR	4	3	4	5	4	4	5	3	4	36
RICK 8	5	3	4	5	5	5	5	3	5	40
PETER 10	5	3	5	6	5	4	5	4	4	41
+/-										
KEITH 14	4	4	5	5	5	4	6	4	4	41
JOE 6	4	3	4	5	5	4	6	4	3	38
PAR	4	3	4	5	4	4	5	3	4	36
HANDICAP	7	15	3	11	17	5	1	13	9	
RED COURSE RATING 71.0	331	100	310	462	304	355	484	110	310	2766
DATE:	SCORER:									

A Kickers Replay event is scored just as an Individual Stroke Play event. In this example the rules for the day allow three shots to be replayed by each player. As you can see on the card,

recommended that the replays that are allowed are not used up too early in the round. The player should feel confident that when he takes a replay he will definitely be able to improve upon the shot that was originally played.

This event is a lot of fun for the players because so often when a poor shot is played a person's first thought is to wish they had a chance to do better. When you play a Kickers Replay you are allowed to do just that and have the excitement of (hopefully) correcting the mistake.

10	11	12	13	14	15	16	17	18	IN	TOT	HCP	NET
515	197	380	390	429	230	481	501	448	3571	7036		
475	163	351	350	382	197	426	465	428	3237	6366		
6	18	14	8	16	4	2	10	12				
5	3	4	4	4	3	4	5	4	36	72		
5	3	4✓5	4	3	5	4✓4	37	77	8	69		
5	4	5	3'	4	3	4✓6	5	39	80	10	70	
6	4	4✓5	5	4	4	7	5	44	85	14	71	
5	2✓4	5	4	3	4✓5	5	37	75	6	69		
5	3	4	4	4	3	5	5	5	38	74		
6	18	4	10	16	2	12	8	14				
420	141	333	299	346	166	398	434	398	2935	5701		

ATTEST:
CHECK TEES PLAYED: ☐ BLUE   ☐ WHITE   ☐ RED

each player has placed a checkmark on the holes where they used one of their replays so that they can keep track of their allocation with a quick glance at the card.

REPLAY COMPETITION

This is a different event to try that will be fun for everyone! Instead of deducting handicap at the end of the round, all players will be able to replay shots during the round at any time. Each player is allowed to replay a number of shots equal to three-quarters of his handicap. If a shot is replayed, it must be used even if the result is worse than the original shot. Also, you are only allowed to replay a shot once.

The fun of this event is deciding when to replay shots. To make sure that the number of replayed shots you have are not

HOLE		1	2	3	4	5	6	7	8	9	OUT
BLUE COURSE RATING 73.5		372	216	413	525	357	436	568	182	396	3465
WHITE COURSE RATING 70.0		349	165	350	492	348	395	517	160	353	3129
HANDICAP		7	13	3	9	17	5	1	15	11	
PAR		4	3	4	5	4	4	5	3	4	36
JOE	16	4	4	5	5	4	5	5	4	5	41
+/-											
PETER	8	4	3	5	5	4	5	4	3	5	38
PAR		4	3	4	5	4	4	5	3	4	36
HANDICAP		7	15	3	11	17	5	1	13	9	
RED COURSE RATING 71.0		331	100	310	462	304	355	484	110	310	2766
DATE:	SCORER:										

In a Replay Competition, instead of deducting handicap at the end of the round, players are allowed to replay any shot during the round. They are allowed three-quarters of their handicap

used up too early in the round you must pick the shots you choose to replay carefully, so that you have something to fall back on if you hit a poor shot near the end of the round.

This is a great format to use in early-season tournaments when most players have not been playing too much and would welcome the opportunity to undo their mistakes. All golfers at one point in time say to themselves after a poor shot "I wish I had that shot over again." This format lets everyone do that and improve upon their mistakes.

	10	11	12	13	14	15	16	17	18	IN	TOT	HCP	NET
	515	197	380	390	429	230	481	501	448	3571	7036		
	475	163	351	350	382	197	426	465	428	3237	6366		
	6	18	14	8	16	4	2	10	12				
	5	3	4	4	4	3	4	5	4	36	72		
	5	3	4	5	5	3	4	5	5	39	80		
	4	4	4	5	4	4	5	4	5	39	77		
	5	3	4	4	4	3	5	5	5	38	74		
	6	18	4	10	16	2	12	8	14				
	420	141	333	299	346	166	398	434	398	2935	5701		

ATTEST:
CHECK TEES PLAYED: ☐ BLUE ☐ WHITE ☐ RED

in replayed shots. Put a check mark in the scoring grid each time a shot is replayed so it is easy to see how many shots you have used up.

PART II MATCH PLAY

INDIVIDUAL MATCH PLAY

Golf has been played under the Match Play system for hundreds of years. It is a very popular form of the game at the club level because it involves head-to-head competition. Match Play is played by holes instead of total score: the winner of the match is the player who takes the most holes during the round.

In Match Play the player who holes out in fewer strokes than his opponent wins that hole. The hole is said to be halved if both players hole out in the same number of strokes. When one player is ahead more holes than there are left to play, the match is over. Because the total gross score for a round does not count at all, it is possible for a player to take several more strokes during the round than his opponent and still beat him in the number of holes won.

Match Play tournaments at the club level usually are played using each player's handicap. The player having the lower handicap will give the player with the higher handicap the number of strokes equal to the difference in their handicaps. The higher handicap player will receive these strokes on the hardest holes on the course (these are designated in order in the "handicap" row on the scorecard). For example, a player with a 9 handicap would give his opponent, a 16 handicap, seven strokes—one stroke each on the seven hardest holes of the course, as designated in the handicap row. If there were a difference of more than 18 strokes between the two players, the higher handicap player would receive two strokes per hole on the number of holes equal to the difference of their handicaps minus eighteen.

When playing those holes the player allowing the strokes, Bill, would have to beat his opponent, Tom, by two strokes gross to win the hole. For instance, if Bill had a 4 on a hole and Tom had a 6, the stroke Tom receives would reduce his score to a net 5 and Bill would still win the hole. However, if

HOLE	1	2	3	4	5	6	7	8	9	OUT
BLUE COURSE RATING 73.5	372	216	413	525	357	436	568	182	396	3465
WHITE COURSE RATING 70.0	349	165	350	492	348	395	517	160	353	3129
HANDICAP	7	13	3	9	17	5	1	15	11	
PAR	4	3	4	5	4	4	5	3	4	36
BILL 9	4	3	5	5	6	4	5	2	5	39
										+1
+/-	+	o	o	+	—	—	o	+	o	
Tom 16	6'	3	6'	6	5	4'	6'	4	5	45
PAR	4	3	4	5	4	4	5	3	4	36
HANDICAP	7	15	3	11	17	5	1	13	9	
RED COURSE RATING 71.0	331	100	310	462	304	355	484	110	310	2766
DATE:	SCORER:									

In this match, Tom receives 7 shots because of the difference between his and Bill's handicap. He takes those shots on the 7 most difficult holes as rated in the handicap row on the

Bill has a 5 and Tom has a 6, the hole would be halved because the stroke Tom received would give him a net score equal to Bill's. If both players take a 5 on the hole, Tom would win the hole with a net 4.

The rules that apply to Match Play under the Rules of Golf differ in many respects from the rules used for a Stroke Play event. You should become familiar with the rules that apply to Match Play because in many situations the rules can help you out. (See Appendix B, Rules of Golf: Differences between Stroke and Match Play.)

Match Play is a great game for all levels of players. The fact that you have to play head to head against someone in your group will inspire your competitive instincts and often times will produce your best golf scores ever!

10	11	12	13	14	15	16	17	18	IN	TOT	HCP	NET
515	197	380	390	429	230	481	501	448	3571	7036		
475	163	351	350	382	197	426	465	428	3237	6366		
6	18	14	8	16	4	2	10	12				
5	3	4	4	4	3	4	5	4	36	72		
5	4	3	4	5	3	4	6	5	39	78		
−	+	o	o	o	−	o	−	o				
5'	4	4	4	5	3'	5'	5	5	40	85 (+1)		
										+2		
5	3	4	4	4	3	5	5	5	38	74		
6	18	4	10	16	2	12	8	14				
420	141	333	299	346	166	398	434	398	2935	5701		

ATTEST:
CHECK TEES PLAYED: ☐ BLUE   ☐ WHITE   ☐ RED

scorecard. Tom wins the match by one stroke because he won five holes during the match and Bill only won four.

FOUR BALL
MATCH PLAY

In Four Ball Match Play two players team up against two opponents with each team's best ball counting on each hole. The team that wins the most holes in the course of the round is the victor. Thus, a match could be over before the end of eighteen holes if one team is up more holes than there are left to play.

To use handicaps in this event, start by using the player with the lowest handicap as a baseline. Simply deduct his handicap from all the other players' handicaps. The lowest player does not get any handicap strokes and the other players are allowed the difference of their handicap minus the low player's handicap. Each player receives his strokes on holes in the order that the holes fall in the handicap row on the scorecard.

In the example match, Joe is a 6 handicap, Chuck is a 12, Pete is an 8, and Harry is a 15. Joe is the low handicap, so he will play at scratch and give 6 shots to his partner Chuck and 2 and 9

HOLE		1	2	3	4	5	6	7	8	9	OUT
BLUE COURSE RATING 73.5		372	216	413	525	357	436	568	182	396	3465
WHITE COURSE RATING 70.0		349	165	350	492	348	395	517	160	353	3129
HANDICAP		7	13	3	9	17	5	1	15	11	
PAR		4	3	4	5	4	4	5	3	4	36
JOE	6	4	3	5	4	5	5	5	3	4	38
CHUCK	12	5	4	5'	6	5	5'	6'	4	6	46
+/-		0	+	+	0	-	0	-	+	0	+1
PETE	8	5	4	5	5	4	4	5'	4	4	40
HARRY	15	5'	5	6'	5'	5	5'	6'	5	6	48
PAR		4	3	4	5	4	4	5	3	4	36
HANDICAP		7	15	3	11	17	5	1	13	9	
RED COURSE RATING 71.0		331	100	310	462	304	355	484	110	310	2766
DATE:		SCORER:									

Joe and Chuck win this match two up with one hole to play because through 17 holes they

shots to their opponents Pete and Harry, respectively.

On the first hole Harry (who gets a handicap stroke here) scores a 5, which becomes a net 4. This ties Joe's gross 4, so the first hole is halved. On the second hole Joe scores a gross 3 to win the hole since no shots were given and neither Pete or Harry could tie Joe. Look over the remainder of the scorecard and you will see how the strokes are used and how the score is kept. Ultimately Joe and Chuck win the match two holes up with one hole to play.

Four Ball Match Play brings out a competitive spirit of team play—it's you against them. You can have a few bad holes, and still be in the match providing your partner has kept pace with your opponents.

As in Individual Match Play, the rules are somewhat different from Stroke Play. See Appendix B to become familiar with these so you can play the game correctly.

	10	11	12	13	14	15	16	17	18	IN	TOT	HCP	NET
	515	197	380	390	429	230	481	501	448	3571	7036		
	475	163	351	350	382	197	426	465	428	3237	6366		
	6	18	14	8	16	4	2	10	12				
	5	3	4	4	4	3	4	5	4	36	72		
	4	3	5	4	5	4	5	5					
	5'	4	5	4	6	3'	5'	6					
	o	+	o	o	—	+	o						
	5	4	5	5	4	3	5'	5					
	5'	5	5	5'	5	4'	6'	6					
	5	3	4	4	4	3	5	5	5	38	74		
	6	18	4	10	16	2	12	8	14				
	420	141	333	299	346	166	398	434	398	2935	5701		

ATTEST:
CHECK TEES PLAYED: ☐ BLUE   ☐ WHITE   ☐ RED

have won two more holes than Pete and Harry.

MATCH PLAY VS. PAR

Players in this game use their net score on each hole in a match against par. Unlike playing a match with one of your opponents, you play a match with par on all of the holes. The winner of this event is the player who obtains the highest score in the plus column at the end of the round.

In scoring this type of event, the number of holes that you lose to par is deducted from the number of holes that you beat

HOLE	1	2	3	4	5	6	7	8	9	OUT
BLUE COURSE RATING 73.5	372	216	413	525	357	436	568	182	396	3465
WHITE COURSE RATING 70.0	349	165	350	492	348	395	517	160	353	3129
HANDICAP	7	13	3	9	17	5	1	15	11	
PAR	4	3	4	5	4	4	5	3	4	36
Joe 16	5'	3'	6'	6'	4	6'	6'	3'	4'	43
	0	+	−	0	0	−	0	+	+	+1
+/−										
Sam 11	5'	3	4'	4'	5	5'	6'	3	5'	40
	0	0	+	+	−	0	0	0	0	+1
PAR	4	3	4	5	4	4	5	3	4	36
HANDICAP	7	15	3	11	17	5	1	13	9	
RED COURSE RATING 71.0	331	100	310	462	304	355	484	110	310	2766
DATE:	SCORER:									

In Match Play vs. Par your opponent is par on each hole. The winner of this event is the player

par. Holes in which you tie par are not figured into the scoring.

In the example, Joe and Sam receive their full handicaps as they fall on the card in the handicap row. They are not playing against each other on a hole-by-hole basis, only on the final total of their score versus par over the whole round. Joe would be the winner since he ended his round one up against par and Sam played even to par.

10	11	12	13	14	15	16	17	18	IN	TOT	HCP	NET
515	197	380	390	429	230	481	501	448	3571	7036		
475	163	351	350	382	197	426	465	428	3237	6366		
6	18	14	8	16	4	2	10	12				
5	3	4	4	4	3	4	5	4	36	72		
5'	4	5'	5'	4'	5'	6'	6'	4'	44	87		
+	−	0	0	+	−	−	0	+	0	+1		
6'	3	4	5'	4	5'	5'	6'	4	42	82		
0	0	0	0	0	−	0	0	0	−1	0		
5	3	4	4	4	3	5	5	5	38	74		
6	18	4	10	16	2	12	8	14				
420	141	333	299	346	166	398	434	398	2935	5701		

ATTEST:
CHECK TEES PLAYED: ☐ BLUE   ☐ WHITE   ☐ RED

who is the most "up" on par after 18 holes.

FOUR BALL
BEST BALL VS. PAR

This competition is a combination of the Match Play vs. Par and Four Ball Best Ball events. As in Four Ball Best Ball, two players act as partners; as in a Match Play vs. Par event, they play against par as their opponent. The team that wins the most holes in its match against par wins.

This event is most often played on a net, or handicap, basis. Each player receives the appropriate number of strokes according to the rankings of holes on the handicap row of the scorecard. In a separate row you keep track of how the team does against par by marking down a plus sign if you win the hole or a minus sign if you lose the hole. Holes that are halved against par are not counted in the final reckoning.

HOLE		1	2	3	4	5	6	7	8	9	OUT
BLUE COURSE RATING 73.5		372	216	413	525	357	436	568	182	396	3465
WHITE COURSE RATING 70.0		349	165	350	492	348	395	517	160	353	3129
HANDICAP		7	13	3	9	17	5	1	15	11	
PAR		4	3	4	5	4	4	5	3	4	36
SEAN	10	5'	4	5'	5'	5	5'	6'	3	5	
BOB	17	6'	3'	6'	6'	6'	6'	5'	3'	6'	
+/-			+		+	–		+	+	–	+2
PAR		4	3	4	5	4	4	5	3	4	36
HANDICAP		7	15	3	11	17	5	1	13	9	
RED COURSE RATING 71.0		331	100	310	462	304	355	484	110	310	2766
DATE:	SCORER:										

In Four Ball Best Ball vs. Par the team's best ball is counted in its match against par. The

To help speed up play it is good etiquette to pick up your ball once it is impossible for you to do better than your partner's score.

Examine the sample scorecard below to see how to score this game. On the first hole Sean had a 5, which becomes a net 4 (since Sean gets a handicap stroke on the first hole). Therefore, they have halved the first hole. On the second hole, Bob had a 3 and receives a shot for a net 2. Since Bob's net score is one better than par their team gets a plus for the hole. If you look on to the fifth hole you will note that neither player's net score equalled or bettered par so in the third row a minus was recorded for the team. By totaling the number of holes that they beat par on and subtracting the number of holes that par beat their best ball, Sean and Bill wound up plus 5 vs. par for the day.

	10	11	12	13	14	15	16	17	18	IN	TOT	HCP	NET
	515	197	380	390	429	230	481	501	448	3571	7036		
	475	163	351	350	382	197	426	465	428	3237	6366		
	6	18	14	8	16	4	2	10	12				
	5	3	4	4	4	3	4	5	4	36	72		
	5'	4	5	5'	4	3'	4'	7'	5				
	6'	4	5'	6'	5'	4'	5'	5'	5'				
	+	−				+	+	+		+3	+5		
	5	3	4	4	4	3	5	5	5	38	74		
	6	18	4	10	16	2	12	8	14				
	420	141	333	299	346	166	398	434	398	2935	5701		

ATTEST:
CHECK TEES PLAYED: ☐ BLUE ☐ WHITE ☐ RED

team that is the most "up" on par after 18 holes is the winner.

BISQUE PAR COMPETITION

This is an interesting variation of Match Play vs. Par competition where the players are allowed to allocate their full handicap in any way they would like during the round. At each tee the players must decide how many of their strokes they would like to take, if any, on that particular hole.

This event can be a lot of fun since you are allowed to use your handicap strokes in any manner you wish. If there are some holes that always give you trouble you can take more strokes so that you can have a better change at beating or matching par. Conversely, on holes that you normally do well on you may choose not to use any of your strokes, saving them for a later

HOLE		1	2	3	4	5	6	7	8	9	OUT
BLUE COURSE RATING 73.5		372	216	413	525	357	436	568	182	396	3465
WHITE COURSE RATING 70.0		349	165	350	492	348	395	517	160	353	3129
HANDICAP		7	13	3	9	17	5	1	15	11	
PAR		4	3	4	5	4	4	5	3	4	36
JOE	*10*	5'	3'	4	5'	5	5'	7'	3	5'	42
			+		+	–		–			0
+/–											
PETER	*24*	5"	5"	6'	6'	5"	4"	7'	5'	5'	48
		+		–		+	+	–	–		0
PAR		4	3	4	5	4	4	5	3	4	36
HANDICAP		7	15	3	11	17	5	1	13	9	
RED COURSE RATING 71.0		331	100	310	462	304	355	484	110	310	2766
DATE:		SCORER:									

In this form of Match Play vs. Par event the player is allowed to allocate his strokes in any manner he pleases during the course of the round. As in Match Play vs. Par the winner is

hole. The players must give some thought to the use of their strokes to be sure that they do not use them up too early in the round and have to play the last few holes without the benefit of any strokes.

In the example provided you can see that Joe and Peter have used their strokes in the manner that they felt was best for them. In playing this type of event it is a good idea to have some sort of plan for using up the handicap strokes you are entitled to before you tee off the first hole. However, since you do not declare how many strokes you will use until you get to each tee, some adjustments can be made depending on the way you are playing that particular day.

10	11	12	13	14	15	16	17	18	IN	TOT	HCP	NET
515	197	380	390	429	230	481	501	448	3571	7036		
475	163	351	350	382	197	426	465	428	3237	6366		
6	18	14	8	16	4	2	10	12				
5	3	4	4	4	3	4	5	4	36	72		
5	3	5'	5'	4	5'	3	6'	4	40	82		
				–	+				0	0		
6"	3'	6'	5'	5'	4'	6"	6'	5'	46	94		
+	+	–					+		+2	+2		
5	3	4	4	4	3	5	5	5	38	74		
6	18	4	10	16	2	12	8	14				
420	141	333	299	346	166	398	434	398	2935	5701		

ATTEST:
CHECK TEES PLAYED: ☐ BLUE   ☐ WHITE   ☐ RED

the player who is the most "up" on par after 18 holes.

HIGH AND LOW BALL

In this variation of Four Ball Match Play two points are involved on each hole. One point is awarded to the team that scores the best on the hole. A point is deducted from the team that has the highest score on a hole. If there is a tie for either the low ball or the high ball no points are distributed.

This game can be played either gross or net. When played in the net format strokes are allocated off of the low player's handicap (the low handicap player gives each of the other players in the group the difference between their handicaps).

This is an exciting game to play, because every shot counts for all players. Unlike playing best ball, all players must play out every hole since high scores as well as the low scores figure into this game. It is important to watch how your opponents stand throughout each hole so that you can plan to be the low ball and never be the high ball.

HOLE		1	2	3	4	5	6	7	8	9	OUT
BLUE COURSE RATING 73.5		372	216	413	525	357	436	568	182	396	3465
WHITE COURSE RATING 70.0		349	165	350	492	348	395	517	160	353	3129
HANDICAP		7	13	3	9	17	5	1	15	11	
PAR		4	3	4	5	4	4	5	3	4	36
BILL	6	4	3	5	5	5	4	5	3	4	
PETER	9	4	4	5'	5	5	6	5'	4	4	
+/-		+1	0	0	+1	-1	0	+1	-1	+2	+3
JOHN	8	5	3	4	6	4	5	5'	3	5	
BRIAN	14	5'	4	6'	5	5	6'	7'	3	6	
PAR		4	3	4	5	4	4	5	3	4	36
HANDICAP		7	15	3	11	17	5	1	13	9	
RED COURSE RATING 71.0		331	100	310	462	304	355	484	110	310	2766
DATE:		SCORER:									

In a High and Low Ball competition your team wins a point if either partner has the low score on the hole. You lose a point to your opponents if you or your partner has the high score

In the example, Bill is the low handicap in the group, so the other players stroke off of his ball. Therefore, Peter receives 3 strokes, John receives 2 strokes and Brian receives 8 strokes. On the scorecard Bill, the scorekeeper of the group, keeps track of how his team is doing against John and Brian by writing down the points won or lost in the middle row. As you can see, Bill and Peter win the match by finishing the 18 holes one point up over their opponents.

On the first hole Bill and Peter win one point because John had the high score of 5 and the other players had 4 each (this was one of Brian's stroke holes, so his 5 became a net 4 to tie Bill and Peter for low ball). If you look at the fifth hole Bill and Peter lose a point because John had the low ball, a 4, and the other three players tied with 5's for the high ball. Look over the remainder of the scorecard to get a feel for how to score this event.

	10	11	12	13	14	15	16	17	18	IN	TOT	HCP	NET
	515	197	380	390	429	230	481	501	448	3571	7036		
	475	163	351	350	382	197	426	465	428	3237	6366		
	6	18	14	8	16	4	2	10	12				
	5	3	4	4	4	3	4	5	4	36	72		
	5	3	5	3	5	3	5	5	5				
	6	3	4	6	4	5	5'	6	5				
	-2	+1	0	0	0	-1	0	+1	-1	-2	+1		
	4	3	5	4	4	4	5'	5	4				
	6'	4	4	5'	5	4'	6'	7	5				
	5	3	4	4	4	3	5	5	5	38	74		
	6	18	4	10	16	2	12	8	14				
	420	141	333	299	346	166	398	434	398	2935	5701		

ATTEST:
CHECK TEES PLAYED: ☐ BLUE ☐ WHITE ☐ RED

on the hole. As in Four Ball Match Play players receive their strokes off the low handicap member of the group.

DROP OUT

This competition is a variation of individual Match Play vs. Par where the winner is the player who can go the furthest into the round before losing a hole to par. As in Match Play vs. Par, each player's full handicap is used as the shots fall on the scorecard in the handicap row. In the event two or more players tie in the number of holes they go before losing to par, the player with the lowest net score for the entire round is declared the winner.

Since you drop out of this event once you have failed to match par on a hole, it is suggested that this event be played in conjunction with some other event. Since it is likely that

HOLE		1	2	3	4	5	6	7	8	9	OUT
BLUE COURSE RATING 73.5		372	216	413	525	357	436	568	182	396	3465
WHITE COURSE RATING 70.0		349	165	350	492	348	395	517	160	353	3129
HANDICAP		7	13	3	9	17	5	1	15	11	
PAR		4	3	4	5	4	4	5	3	4	36
ART	4	4	3	4'	4	4	5	5'	4	3	36
+/-				+		-					
JACK	10	5'	3	4'	6'	4	5'	4'	3	4	38
				+				+			
PAR		4	3	4	5	4	4	5	3	4	36
HANDICAP		7	15	3	11	17	5	1	13	9	
RED COURSE RATING 71.0		331	100	310	462	304	355	484	110	310	2766
DATE:	SCORER:										

In the example, Jack would be the winner since the first hole he lost in his match against par

most players will lose to par early in the round, it is a good idea to stage some other golfing event at the same time to keep their interest going.

The strategy in this tournament is a little different because the reward is not for the most holes won; it is for the player who can go the furthest without losing to par. Therefore, each hole should be played with one thought in mind: Do not let par beat me! Most often the conservative player who knows when to take risks and when to hold back is the player who will do well in this event.

	10	11	12	13	14	15	16	17	18	IN	TOT	HCP	NET
	515	197	380	390	429	230	481	501	448	3571	7036		
	475	163	351	350	382	197	426	465	428	3237	6366		
	6	18	14	8	16	4	2	10	12				
	5	3	4	4	4	3	4	5	4	36	72		
	5	3	5	4	5	3'	4'	4	5	38	74		
	6'	4	5	5'	4	4'	6'	5'	4	43	81		
	5	3	4	4	4	3	5	5	5	38	74		
	6	18	4	10	16	2	12	8	14				
	420	141	333	299	346	166	398	434	398	2935	5701		

ATTEST:
CHECK TEES PLAYED: ☐ BLUE   ☐ WHITE   ☐ RED

was the 11th hole and Art lost to par on the 6th hole.

SKINS GAME

This contest has become very popular in the last few years with the growth of the high-stakes Skins Game televised each fall featuring stars of professional golf. The game is very simple: two tie, all tie. If a player has a lower score on a hole than the other players, he wins a "skin."

This game can be played within one group or the whole field of a large tournament. It can be played on a gross or net basis. When played on a net basis, each player should deduct his full handicap according to the scorecard's handicap rankings.

The Skins Game can be played two ways. In Straight Skins each "skin" or hole won would be worth the same number of points. In Carryover Skins if a hole is tied the next hole is worth two skins; if that hole is tied the following hole would be worth three skins, and so on.

In the sample scorecard the circled holes are skins. This group is playing gross skins. You can see on the first hole that even though Bill and Al score higher than George and Randy, they do not lose any

HOLE	1	2	3	4	5	6	7	8	9	OUT
BLUE COURSE RATING 73.5	372	216	413	525	357	436	568	182	396	3465
WHITE COURSE RATING 70.0	349	165	350	492	348	395	517	160	353	3129
HANDICAP	7	13	3	9	17	5	1	15	11	
PAR	4	3	4	5	4	4	5	3	4	36
BILL	5	3	5	5	4	3	5	3	③	36
GEORGE	4	4	4	5	4	5	5	3	4	38
+/−										
AL	6	3	4	④	5	3	5	5	5	40
RANDY	4	②	4	6	5	5	5	4	5	40
PAR	4	3	4	5	4	4	5	3	4	36
HANDICAP	7	15	3	11	17	5	1	13	9	
RED COURSE RATING 71.0	331	100	310	462	304	355	484	110	310	2766
DATE:	SCORER:									

When playing Skins in your own group, just circle a hole when one of the players has scored lower than all the others and won a "skin." When playing Skins with a large field a big

points since George and Randy tie the hole with par. On the second hole Randy gets a skin because he has the lowest score and no one ties him. If this group had been playing carryovers Randy's 2 on the second hole would have been worth two skins, and Bill's 3 on the ninth hole would have been worth five skins. In looking over the scorecard you can see even though there was a fairly large difference in the players' scores, there was not a big difference in the number of skins won.

Skins is a great game, especially within a foursome, because there can be a lot of pressure on you to tie if one player has already holed out and you are the last one in the group with a chance to tie his score. Also, your game plan on some holes may be different from how you might normally play those holes. If you see the fellows you are playing with hit into trouble you may play a safer route. On the other hand, if someone you are playing with hits a great shot, you might be tempted to try a risky shot in an effort to tie or beat your opponent.

	10	11	12	13	14	15	16	17	18	IN	TOT	HCP	NET
	515	197	380	390	429	230	481	501	448	3571	7036		
	475	163	351	350	382	197	426	465	428	3237	6366		
	6	18	14	8	16	4	2	10	12				
	5	3	4	4	4	3	4	5	4	36	72		
	5	3	5	4	5	(3)	4	5	4	38	74		
	5	3	5	4	(4)	4	4	4	(3)	36	74		
	4	3	6	4	6	4	4	5	4	40	80		
	4	4	5	4	5	5	4	4	5	40	80		
	5	3	4	4	4	3	5	5	5	38	74		
	6	18	4	10	16	2	12	8	14				
	420	141	333	299	346	166	398	434	398	2935	5701		

ATTEST:
CHECK TEES PLAYED: ☐ BLUE   ☐ WHITE   ☐ RED

scoresheet where all players' hole-by-hole scores can be listed will make determining winners much easier.

ROUND-ROBIN

In a Round-Robin Tournament each player, at some point during the course of the tournament, plays a head-to-head match against every other player. The winner is the player who has won the most matches. These events are most often played under Match Play with full handicap.

In setting up a Round-Robin Tournament some advance planning is needed so that it will run smoothly. First, a schedule of matches should be published so that each player knows well in advance whom he is to play with and when.

	MATCH 1	MATCH 2	TOTAL	MATCH 3	MATCH 4	TOTAL	MATCH 5	MATCH 6	TOTAL
TEAM 1									
TEAM 2									
TEAM 3									
TEAM 4									
TEAM 5									
TEAM 6									

1 vs. 2	1 vs. 3	1 vs. 4	1 vs. 5	1 vs. 6
3 vs. 4	2 vs. 6	3 vs. 6	4 vs. 6	2 vs. 4
5 vs. 6	4 vs. 5	2 vs. 5	2 vs. 3	3 vs. 5

Below each match column is listed the order in which teams play the Round-Robin format. The sixth and final match is based on the team standings after the first five matches have been completed.

Second, you need a time period within which each scheduled match must be completed, particularly for a season-long event. [Generally, in a season-long tournament if a player cannot play his scheduled opponent within the time limit he forfeits that match but may continue in the tournament for the remainder of the season.]

Round-Robin is also a good format for a weekend Member-Guest where the golfers play as teams rather than as individuals. You can set the tournament up in flights of six teams. Each team plays a nine-hole match against every other team, gaining one point for each hole won, and losing one point for each hole lost. The first two days the flights play two matches per day. The third day the fifth match is played in the morning. When that match is done all six teams in a flight have played each other once.

At this point the two teams with the highest point total play one more match, as do the teams in third and fourth place, and the teams in fifth and sixth place. At the end of this final match the team that has won the most points or holes for the weekend is the winner. If two teams tie, the winner is the team that won in their head-to-head competition.

The Round-Robin tournament lends itself very well to a weekend Member-Guest affair, where you want to encourage both a competitive and social golfing experience for all of the entrants. It's a great way to get people to meet each other, since players who would not usually play with each other have to in order to complete the tournament. A Round-Robin format is also a natural for a season-long event for a business, men's, or ladies' golf league.

LADDER TOURNAMENT

At the start of a Ladder Tournament the names of all the entrants are listed in descending order according to their handicaps. A player can challenge any one of the three players who appear above him on the "ladder." If the challenger wins, his name is moved up to the spot occupied by the player whom he beat and that player's name is moved down to the spot formerly held by the challenger. From his new position the challenger can challenge any one of the next three players higher up on the ladder. If, on the

PLAYER 1
PLAYER 2
PLAYER 3
PLAYER 4
PLAYER 5
PLAYER 6
PLAYER 7
PLAYER 8
PLAYER 9
PLAYER 10
PLAYER 11
PLAYER 12

In the Ladder Tournament players may challenge any of the three players above on the "ladder." For example, Player 10 could challenge either number 7, 8, or 9.

other hand, a player who initiates a challenge loses the match, the players' names remain in the same position. Any player who loses is not allowed to challenge a player higher up until he has been able to successfully defend his position from a challenger below him on the "ladder."

While you can play this tournament under many different formats, the most common one to use is Match Play. If the participants have widely varying abilities you may decide to use handicaps. It can be played as either a 9- or 18-hole event. A time limit should be established that will penalize players one rung on the ladder if they do not play at least one match within the set amount of time.

This is a great season-long event when it's difficult to get a whole group together at the same time to play on a regular basis. The players can pick whom they want to play and set convenient times to get together. At the end of the season, you can also stage an ending match for final position: the two top golfers play off for first and second place, the next two for third and fourth, and so on down the ladder.

PART III POINT COMPETITIONS

POINT COMPETITION

In this type of event players vie for points rather than for holes or aggregate score. Eight points are given for a net eagle, six points for a net birdie, four points for a net par and two points for a net bogey.

Players are allowed their full number of handicap strokes, which are to be used as the hole rankings fall on the scorecard's handicap stroke row. Instead of playing for a gross score, points are awarded for each hole, then totaled at the end of the round. The player compiling the largest total wins.

This is a fun event to play, because you can have some bad holes and not knock yourself out of the tournament. Your point total can change very quickly if you play well on just a few holes.

HOLE		1	2	3	4	5	6	7	8	9	OUT	
BLUE COURSE RATING 73.5		372	216	413	525	357	436	568	182	396	3465	
WHITE COURSE RATING 70.0		349	165	350	492	348	395	517	160	353	3129	
HANDICAP		7	13	3	9	17	5	1	15	11		
PAR		4	3	4	5	4	4	5	3	4	36	
ANDY	6	6	4	5'	6	6	4'	6'	3	4		
POINTS			2	4	2			6	4	4	4	26
+/-												
SAM	14	4'	3'	5'	6'	6	5'	6'	5	5'		
POINTS		6	6	4	4			4	4		4	32
PAR		4	3	4	5	4	4	5	3	4	36	
HANDICAP		7	15	3	11	17	5	1	13	9		
RED COURSE RATING 71.0		331	100	310	462	304	355	484	110	310	2766	
DATE:		SCORER:										

In this event points can add up quickly. A few good holes can bring a struggling player back into competition with the rest of the players. Never count yourself out when playing this

In the sample scorecard you can see that Andy did not play well on the first nine holes and was six points behind Sam. But, by playing better on the second nine, he made up those points to overtake Sam's point total for the whole round.

In this format of play you do not lose points for a bad hole. Therefore, it is to your benefit to play some risky shots. If you do get into situations where you need a miracle shot to get points, go for it—you have nothing to lose. Remember, in the interest of fast play, you should pick up your ball once you are beyond bogey and cannot score any points.

	10	11	12	13	14	15	16	17	18	IN	TOT	HCP	NET
	515	197	380	390	429	230	481	501	448	3571	7036		
	475	163	351	350	382	197	426	465	428	3237	6366		
	6	18	14	8	16	4	2	10	12				
	5	3	4	4	4	3	4	5	4	36	72		
	4'	3	5	5	4	4'	5'	4	5				
	8	4	2	2	4	4	4	6	2	36	62		
	6'	5	5'	5'	5	6'	5'	7'	5'				
	4		4	4	2		4	2	4	24	56		
	5	3	4	4	4	3	5	5	5	38	74		
	6	18	4	10	16	2	12	8	14				
	420	141	333	299	346	166	398	434	398	2935	5701		

ATTEST:
CHECK TEES PLAYED: ☐ BLUE   ☐ WHITE   ☐ RED

method of scoring!

QUOTA GAME

This is a very popular event where a couple of good scores can add quickly to your point total. The scoring format for this event awards large points for eagles and birdies, so a few good holes can add points in a hurry.

The player's "quota" is determined by deducting his handicap from 36. The resulting number is the point total that the player must score to reach his quota. The player who exceeds his quota by the most points, or comes the closest to it if no one exceeds his or her total, is the winner.

HOLE	1	2	3	4	5	6	7	8	9	OUT
BLUE COURSE RATING 73.5	372	216	413	525	357	436	568	182	396	3465
WHITE COURSE RATING 70.0	349	165	350	492	348	395	517	160	353	3129
HANDICAP	7	13	3	9	17	5	1	15	11	
PAR	4	3	4	5	4	4	5	3	4	36
HENRY 10	5	3	6	4	5	4	6	4	4	41
QUOTA 26	1	2		4	1	2	1	1	2	14
+/-										
GEORGE 24	5	3	6	5	7	5	7	2	5	45
QUOTA 12	1	2		2		1		4	1	11
PAR	4	3	4	5	4	4	5	3	4	36
HANDICAP	7	15	3	11	17	5	1	13	9	
RED COURSE RATING 71.0	331	100	310	462	304	355	484	110	310	2766
DATE:	SCORER:									

George wins because he exceeded his quota by four more points than did Henry.

Points are scored in the following manner: one point for a bogey, two points for a par, four points for a birdie, and eight points for an eagle.

In the example, Henry is a 10 handicap and George is a 24 handicap, so the quotas that they must attain are, respectively, 26 and 12. At the end of the round, even though George's total is lower than Henry's, George is the winner, because he is six points over his quota and Henry is only two points over his.

10	11	12	13	14	15	16	17	18	IN	TOT	HCP	NET
515	197	380	390	429	230	481	501	448	3571	7036		
475	163	351	350	382	197	426	465	428	3237	6366		
6	18	14	8	16	4	2	10	12				
5	3	4	4	4	3	4	5	4	36	72		
5	2	5	5	4	4	6	5	5	41	82		
2	4	1	1	2	1		2	1	14	28		(+2)
6	4	6	4	7	5	5	5	7	49	94		
1	1		2			1	2		7	18		(+6)
5	3	4	4	4	3	5	5	5	38	74		
6	18	4	10	16	2	12	8	14				
420	141	333	299	346	166	398	434	398	2935	5701		

ATTEST:
CHECK TEES PLAYED: ☐ BLUE   ☐ WHITE   ☐ RED

STABLEFORD

The Stableford format for scoring is one of the oldest forms of play for tournaments that use a point system of scoring. In this event the player accumulates points on a hole-by-hole basis. Points are awarded for the player's net score on each individual hole.

The scoring method is calculated by allocating one point for a net bogey, two points for a net par, three points for a net birdie, and four points for a net eagle. The points are then totaled after each nine and added together to form the 18-hole total. The winner is the player who attains the highest number of points.

In the example card, the scores for Paul and Wayne are shown for each hole and the number of points awarded are shown in the row below their actual score. The holes for which they deduct their handicap strokes are designated by a slash in the upper right hand corner of the scoring box for that particular hole. Paul is a

HOLE		1	2	3	4	5	6	7	8	9	OUT
BLUE COURSE RATING 73.5		372	216	413	525	357	436	568	182	396	3465
WHITE COURSE RATING 70.0		349	165	350	492	348	395	517	160	353	3129
HANDICAP		7	13	3	9	17	5	1	15	11	
PAR		4	3	4	5	4	4	5	3	4	36
PAUL	12	5'	4	4'	5'	6	5'	5'	4	7'	
POINTS		2	1	3	3		2	3	1		15
+/-											
WAYNE	18	6'	4'	5'	6'	7'	7'	6'	3'	6'	
POINTS		1	2	2	2			2	3	1	13
PAR		4	3	4	5	4	4	5	3	4	36
HANDICAP		7	15	3	11	17	5	1	13	9	
RED COURSE RATING 71.0		331	100	310	462	304	355	484	110	310	2766
DATE:	SCORER:										

In a Stableford Tournament the player's net score on each hole is used in the allocation of

12 handicap so he receives a stroke on the 12 most difficult holes according to the handicap row of the scorecard. Wayne, an 18 handicap, is allowed to deduct a stroke on every hole. In the first row each player enters his gross score on each hole. By going through the scores for each player you can see how the points are awarded for each player's net score in the next row. In this case Paul is the winner because his 18-hole point total is three points higher than Wayne's.

The Stableford format has two major advantages. First, it speeds up play since you need not finish a hole out if the number of strokes you have taken on a hole exceeds a net bogey. The other advantage is that one or two bad holes will not eliminate you from a chance at winning this event. A few good holes later in the round can quickly put you right back in the ball game.

10	11	12	13	14	15	16	17	18	IN	TOT	HCP	NET
515	197	380	390	429	230	481	501	448	3571	7036		
475	163	351	350	382	197	426	465	428	3237	6366		
6	18	14	8	16	4	2	10	12				
5	3	4	4	4	3	4	5	4	36	72		
5'	3	5	7'	4	3'	5'	6'	5'				
3	2	1		2	3	2	2	2	17	32		
6'	4'	5'	6'	7'	4'	4'	6'	5'				
2	2	2	1		2	3	2	2	16	29		
5	3	4	4	4	3	5	5	5	38	74		
6	18	4	10	16	2	12	8	14				
420	141	333	299	346	166	398	434	398	2935	5701		

ATTEST:
CHECK TEES PLAYED: ☐ BLUE   ☐ WHITE   ☐ RED

points. Paul is the winner in this example since he accumulated more points than Wayne.

FOUR BALL
BEST BALL STABLEFORD

The Stableford method of scoring (one point for bogey, two for par, three for birdie, four for eagle) is used in this competition. Two golfers play as partners, each using their full individual handicap as their strokes fall on the scorecard. On each hole, the team member with the best score has his score entered on the card for the team. The team accumulating the most points for the round is the winner.

There is no need for both players' scores to be recorded, so it is customary for players to pick up their ball once it is impossible for them to exceed their partner's points on that hole. This will help speed up play. If all players do this a large number of players can play very quickly.

When a Four Ball Best Ball Stableford or any other event is played with mixed teams of men and women, the women should use their own tees and strokes should be allocated to the women from their own handicap row on the scorecard. In the example, you can see that the

HOLE	1	2	3	4	5	6	7	8	9	OUT
BLUE COURSE RATING 73.5	372	216	413	525	357	436	568	182	396	3465
WHITE COURSE RATING 70.0	349	165	350	492	348	395	517	160	353	3129
HANDICAP	7	13	3	9	17	5	1	15	11	
PAR	4	3	4	5	4	4	5	3	4	36
BILL	10	5'3	6'	5'3	3'	6'	4	5	40	
MARY	27	5"	5"	6"	5'5'	4"8"	3'	6"	47	
+/-										
POINTS		3	2	2	3	3	4	2	3	2	24
PAR	4	3	4	5	4	4	5	3	4	36
HANDICAP	7	15	3	11	17	5	1	13	9	
RED COURSE RATING 71.0	331	100	310	462	304	355	484	110	310	2766
DATE:	SCORER:									

This is an example of a mixed event. Men are allocated their strokes from the handicap row above the scoring grid and women are allocated their strokes from the handicap row below

strokes have been allocated for both the men and the women in the group from the appropriate handicap row.

It is best to mark the stroke holes before the round is started so each player can glance at the card and see at any time where and how many strokes he or she will be getting on the upcoming holes. It is always best for the players to know when each is getting or not getting strokes because this may influence the team's strategy for playing certain holes on the course.

As in a Four Ball Stroke Play tournament it is important that each player be aware of how his partner is doing and choose his shot selection accordingly. When your partner is in good position, take some chances. When he is in trouble use your head and play conservatively so both of you don't end up in trouble and the resulting big number.

10	11	12	13	14	15	16	17	18	IN	TOT	HCP	NET
515	197	380	390	429	230	481	501	448	3571	7036		
475	163	351	350	382	197	426	465	428	3237	6366		
6	18	14	8	16	4	2	10	12				
5	3	4	4	4	3	4	5	4	36	72		
6'	3	5	6'	6	4'	4'	5'	5	44	84		
8"	5'	7"	5'	6'	4"	4'	6"	6'	51	98		
2	2	1	2	1	3	3	3	1	18	42		
5	3	4	4	4	3	5	5	5	38	74		
6	18	4	10	16	2	12	8	14				
420	141	333	299	346	166	398	434	398	2935	5701		

ATTEST:
CHECK TEES PLAYED: ☐ BLUE ☐ WHITE ☐ RED

the scoring grid.

FOUR BALL
AGGREGATE STABLEFORD

Another format that Stableford scoring lends itself well to is a Four Ball Aggregate Tournament. This event is scored the same as the other Stableford events described earlier (one point for bogey, two for par, three for birdie, four for eagle). The points each player earns for each hole are added together for an aggregate team score for each hole. The team that has the highest point total for the round is the winner.

In the example scorecard, the scoring of this event is illustrated by keeping Charlie's and Peter's gross score in the first two rows. Note that the holes where they are to receive handicap strokes are designated with slash marks in the upper right hand corner. The team's points are kept in a third row, which is then totaled for the team's score.

Looking at the first hole you see that both players had bogey fives. Peter receives a stroke on the hole, so he scores two points for his

HOLE		1	2	3	4	5	6	7	8	9	OUT
BLUE COURSE RATING 73.5		372	216	413	525	357	436	568	182	396	3465
WHITE COURSE RATING 70.0		349	165	350	492	348	395	517	160	353	3129
HANDICAP		7	13	3	9	17	5	1	15	11	
PAR		4	3	4	5	4	4	5	3	4	36
CHARLIE	6	5	3	4'	5	6	3'	5'	4	4	39
PETER	15	5'	4'	5'	6'	4	5'	5'	4'	5'	43
+/-											
POINTS		3	4	5	4	2	6	6	3	4	37
PAR		4	3	4	5	4	4	5	3	4	36
HANDICAP		7	15	3	11	17	5	1	13	9	
RED COURSE RATING 71.0		331	100	310	462	304	355	484	110	310	2766
DATE:	SCORER:										

The points earned by each player on every hole are added together in a Four Ball Aggregate Stableford event to be the team's score. To do well in this event it is important for each player

net par. Charlie, who receives no handicap stroke on this hole, scores one point for his bogey, so the team ends up with three points for the first hole. On the second hole Charlie has a par three with no strokes and Peter has a bogey four with a stroke. The team total for the second hole is four. Review the remainder of the scores for Charlie and Peter so that you become comfortable in scoring this type of event.

Aggregate tournaments are difficult for the players because every hole must count. In a Best Ball event a few bad holes by one player probably will not hurt the team too much providing his partner does reasonably well on those bad holes. However, when playing an aggregate event every hole for each player must count and a couple of poor holes could knock the team right out of contention. This type of event rewards players who can play a consistent round and who can avoid the kind of trouble that produces devastating high numbers.

10	11	12	13	14	15	16	17	18	IN	TOT	HCP	NET
515	197	380	390	429	230	481	501	448	3571	7036		
475	163	351	350	382	197	426	465	428	3237	6366		
6	18	14	8	16	4	2	10	12				
5	3	4	4	4	3	4	5	4	36	72		
5	2	5	5	4	4	4	4	5	38	77		
5	4	5	5	5	5	5	7	4	45	88		
6	4	3	3	3	3	5	4	4	35	72		
5	3	4	4	4	3	5	5	5	38	74		
6	18	4	10	16	2	12	8	14				
420	141	333	299	346	166	398	434	398	2935	5701		

ATTEST:
CHECK TEES PLAYED: ☐ BLUE   ☐ WHITE   ☐ RED

to score points on each hole and avoid big numbers that do not add points to the team's total.

BINGLE-BANGLE-BUNGLE

In this game three points are awarded on each hole. The first point goes to the player who is first on the putting surface. The second point is awarded to the player who is closest to the hole when all the balls are on the green (it does not matter how many strokes each player has taken). The third and final point goes to the first player to hole out in the group (the continuous putting rule is not allowed when playing this event).

This game can be played within your group in conjunction with other games. It is a good game to play when there is a large difference in ability levels of the players within the group because your score on the hole does not matter in the winning of the points.

For example, a player could be playing a particular hole very poorly and get to the green in a couple of more strokes than his playing partners. By hitting a good chip shot he gets his ball on the green and is closest to the hole to win one point. To go one step further: if all the other players miss their putts and he ends up

HOLE	1	2	3	4	5	6	7	8	9	OUT
BLUE COURSE RATING 73.5	372	216	413	525	357	436	568	182	396	3465
WHITE COURSE RATING 70.0	349	165	350	492	348	395	517	160	353	3129
HANDICAP	7	13	3	9	17	5	1	15	11	
PAR	4	3	4	5	4	4	5	3	4	36
JOE	/	/		/	//		/	/	/	8
CHARLIE		//	/		/	//		/	/	8
+/–										
PETE	/			/			//		/	5
PAUL	/		//	/		/		/		6
PAR	4	3	4	5	4	4	5	3	4	36
HANDICAP	7	15	3	11	17	5	1	13	9	
RED COURSE RATING 71.0	331	100	310	462	304	355	484	110	310	2766
DATE:		SCORER:								

It is easiest to keep the points in Bingle-Bangle-Bungle on a separate scorecard from the one you use for the actual score. The high-point winner would collect the difference in points from

making the longest putt he would win another point. So it is possible to play more strokes on a hole than your playing partners and still score more points than they do.

The strategy and placement of shots is very important in this game. For example, on a short par four it might be to your advantage to lay up off the tee so that you, being "away" on the second shot, will have the first chance to get your ball on the green. In another instance you might intentionally miss the green if one of your playing partners has hit a long shot onto the green that ended up fairly close to the pin. You may not feel that you can best that shot from the distance you are out, but feel confident that you could be inside the closest ball with a good chip shot from just off the green. Knowing your game and the abilities of your opponents are the keys to your shot selection and to doing well in this game.

10	11	12	13	14	15	16	17	18	IN	TOT	HCP	NET
515	197	380	390	429	230	481	501	448	3571	7036		
475	163	351	350	382	197	426	465	428	3237	6366		
6	18	14	8	16	4	2	10	12				
5	3	4	4	4	3	4	5	4	36	72		
/	/	/	//			/	/		7	15		
	//			/		/	//		6	14		
/		/		//	//	/		/	8	13		
/		/	/		/			//	6	12		
5	3	4	4	4	3	5	5	5	38	74		
6	18	4	10	16	2	12	8	14				
420	141	333	299	346	166	398	434	398	2935	5701		

ATTEST:
CHECK TEES PLAYED: ☐ BLUE   ☐ WHITE   ☐ RED

the other players in the group when the round is completed.

PART IV SINGLE SHOT EVENTS AND OTHER GAMES

CLOSEST TO PIN

Closest to Pin can be played between as few as two golfers or the field of a large tournament. On a designated par 3 hole the player who hits the ball closest to the hole in one shot wins.

This is a good add-on event to hold during large tournaments because it gives players who may not be playing well an opportunity to win something based on one good shot. It can keep up the interest of players who are essentially out of the running, rewarding as it does a single, beautiful stroke from tee to green on the designated hole (or holes—you can play for several holes if you wish). And, of course, it can add luster to the ultimate golf shot, a hole in one.

A Closest To Pin contest for a large tournament field should include some sort of measuring device and a sign to record players' distances from the hole set up at the green for the players' convenience. If it is a very large affair you should have someone present to do the measuring and thus speed up the play.

CLOSEST TO LINE

This is another enjoyable add-on competition for a tournament with a large field. On a designated hole a line is drawn down the center of the fairway. The player whose tee shot is the closest to that line wins. The distance the ball goes does not matter, just the distance the ball comes to rest from that line.

Because it is a game of accuracy, this event gives all players a good chance to win, even the players who do not have a powerful game. It emphasizes the fundamentals of golf—a nice smooth swing, solid contact, and a straight shot.

LONG
DRIVE

Long Drive is most often conducted during a large event, but you also could play this game with any size group. On designated holes the player who hits his drive the farthest off the tee in the fairway wins. Long, open holes are the best to use for this event so that all players get a chance to take a hard swing and show off their power game!

When setting up a Long Drive hole in a tournament, signs should be placed on the tee and a note should be made on the rules sheet each player receives prior to teeing off so that all players know where the special events are taking place. A sign that is easy to move should be placed in the fairway that the players can advance themselves if their drive is beyond the location of the sign. A sheet of paper and a pencil should be attached to the sign so the player can mark his name down quickly and not hold up play.

Sometimes, if time is not a constraint, a separate Long Drive competition can be held after play on the driving range. These are a lot of fun and can be a good way to while away the time while the tournament committee is checking and posting the results of the competition held earlier in the day.

FEWEST
PUTTS

Players keep track of the number of strokes taken on the putting green only. The winner is the player who takes the fewest number of putts over the course of a round. Note that only strokes taken on the clipped surface of the green count, even if the putter is used from off the green. This game can be played in conjunction with other events and is a nice add-on event to recognize the individual who had the hottest putter that day.

SANDIES

Sandies rewards good shots from sand bunkers. You get a sandy when you are able to get out of a bunker and hole your next shot (to get up and down in two strokes). At the end of the round the player who has the most sandies collects the difference in his total from that of the other players.

This is a good game to play for those who are confident in their ability to get the ball out of the sand and onto the green close enough to hole out the next shot. It's also good for those who want that extra incentive to develop good sand technique.

You may well ask: Doesn't this game reward golfers who get into the sand a lot? Of course, it's possible; an excellent sand shot player may want to end up in the sand deliberately in order to collect more sandies! But that isn't really in the spirit of the game. This is supposed to be a competition that rewards getting out of trouble, not into it.

FLAG
COMPETITION

In this event each player receives a flag with his name on it. You play until your score is equal to par plus your handicap. When you reach that point you plant your flag in the ground. The winner is the player who advances his flag the farthest along the course. In most cases a few good players will have to play an extra hole or two to meet their quota of strokes.

STRING
TOURNAMENT

Instead of using handicap strokes, each player is given a piece of string equaling, in feet, his or her handicap. The player may move the ball at any time during the course of the round to a more favorable spot. Using the string, the player measures the distance he has moved the ball, then cuts that amount off of the string. You may advance the ball into a hole, away from a tree, or out of a difficult lie. However, once the string is used up you are on your own. So be careful not to use up your string too early in the round.

The strategy in this event is to know your strengths and weaknesses on the course. If, for example, you often have problems with some of the ending holes of the course, it would be wise to use as little of the string as possible until you get by the holes that have been difficult for you in the past.

This is a fun event to try because you must make decisions about your round and how much string to hold on to before you really know what is going to happen. It is quite a challenge to predict and use the right amount of string so that you do not run out too early in the round—or worse yet, have a lot of string left over at the end of the round because you were too conservative in saving it.

ONE
CLUB

Each player is allowed to use only one club to play a round of golf. This can be played as either a gross or net event, and as either a stroke or match competition. You can score according to the rules of almost any of the games described in this book. The difference is that you only get to use that one club.

Many variations of this type of play can be devised that allow the players to carry two or three clubs. Sometimes you are allowed to bring a putter to use on the greens; sometimes you are not. Whatever you decide, it makes for a very interesting event because you must learn to play shots with a club you might not normally use in many different situations.

To play this event well you need to think ahead to the next stroke or two even as you are making a shot. For example, if you are playing with a long club on a course with fast greens, you may want to avoid difficult chip situations. Playing with a shorter club may require careful planning around water hazards and bunkers. Depending on the number of clubs that are allowed, you will need to be flexible and creative in planning your shots.

SHOOT
OUT

This 9-hole event can get ferociously competitive, because the stakes are high on every hole. Ten players start out. On each hole, the player with the high score for that hole is eliminated. If there is a tie for the high score, there is a chip-off between all the players with the high score; the player who ends up farthest from the hole drops out. When you reach the last hole there will be just two players fighting it out to be champion.

This game is best suited for golfers of similar abilities. Most often the winner is the player who uses the best strategy in playing within his game, steadily and without taking chances that could result in a big number. To continue a long way in this game you must be aware of how the other players are doing on each hole and adjust your game to the circumstances. For instance, if one of the players is in trouble, you may want to play more conservatively, especially if you are faced with a difficult shot that you may not be able to pull off. Remember, there is no reward for having the low score on each hole, so it makes sense to look at it from the other side—play to avoid the high score.

MOST THREES, FOURS, FIVES

This event is most often run in conjunction with another tournament and awards prizes to the players who have the most threes, fours and fives on their card. While this is not a championship type of event, it is a fun add-on event to run when you have a large outing.

Scoring this event is quite simple. When the scores are turned in for the main event of the day, the scorers go through all of the cards to count how many threes, fours and fives each player had (it's useful and quicker to have an extra scorer to go through the cards for just this purpose). It can be done on a gross or net basis; as usual, the playing level of the field in the tournament should decide which scoring method will best suit the group of players involved.

Remember that this is intended to be a fun sort of event. You can carry it as far as you like to include most sixes, sevens, eights, etc. Of course, after you get past about sixes or sevens, the prize becomes a more dubious honor!

CROSS COUNTRY COMPETITION

You should play this event when you have the whole course to yourself. Instead of playing the course in the usual order, golfers play a new course that is a mixture of many holes on the course. With a good imagination, an interesting and challenging event can be created.

To make this a successful event, well-planned instructions must be made up for all players so that they know exactly the route they are to take. What makes this event so interesting is that a number of holes can be created on your existing golf course that might require difficult shots over trees or other hazards on the course that normally do not come into play. To make things even more interesting, try to plan out holes so that there are two different ways to play them, so that the players will have to do some thinking and use their imagination to score the best.

Any format for scoring can be used for a Cross Country competition. Some of the best formats to use are some sort of partners event or a scramble. Since most of the shots will be played from different directions and confronting new hazards, some of the players may run into some trouble because they will be hitting many unfamiliar shots. Having a partner to fall back on will make it more enjoyable for all.

APPENDIX A
THE CALLAWAY SYSTEM
OF HANDICAPPING

This system offers a solution to the problem many tournament organizers have when there is a large number of players in the field who do not have established handicaps. Developed by Lionel Callaway, a professional in Pinehurst, North Carolina, the system determines each player's handicap for that day by deducting a set number of his worst holes from his total score.

The following table shows the number of worst holes that may be deducted from a player's gross score. After the total of the worst holes has been determined, an adjustment must be made to the "handicap." This adjustment is indicated in the bottom row of the table. For example, if a player's gross score is 80, the player would first deduct his worst hole, then add two strokes to his total. The seventeenth and eighteenth holes are never deducted.

This is a very good system to use when there are many novice or occasional players in the event that do not have handicaps. It is surprising how close all of the net scores come out. In this event a few bad holes will not hurt you because it is likely that they will be the ones that will be deducted from your score. Therefore, taking some chances and playing aggressive is the game plan to follow.

In the example, the holes that are circled are the worst holes that are totaled to form the player's handicap. The holes that have a circle with a slash are only counted as one-half of that number according to the table. Harry and Rich tie with net 74's. In the case of ties the player with the lower handicap or adjustment should be the winner.

GROSS SCORE

		70	71	72
73	74	75		
76	77	78	79	80
81	82	83	84	85
86	87	88	89	90
91	92	93	94	95
96	97	98	99	100
101	102	103	104	105
106	107	108	109	110
111	112	113	114	115
116	117	118	119	120
121	122	123	124	125
126	127	128	129	130

NUMBER OF WORST HOLES DEDUCTED

Scratch—No Adjustment
½ worst hole plus adjustment
1 worst hole plus adjustment
1½ worst holes plus adjustment
2 worst holes plus adjustment
2½ worst holes plus adjustment
3 worst holes plus adjustment
3½ worst holes plus adjustment
4 worst holes plus adjustment
4½ worst holes plus adjustment
5 worst holes plus adjustment
5½ worst holes plus adjustment
6 worst holes plus adjustment

ADJUSTMENT
Add or Deduct to Handicap

-2	-1	0	+1	+2

HOLE	1	2	3	4	5	6	7	8	9	OUT
BLUE COURSE RATING 73.5	372	216	413	525	357	436	568	182	396	3465
WHITE COURSE RATING 70.0	349	165	350	492	348	395	517	160	353	3129
HANDICAP	7	13	3	9	17	5	1	15	11	
PAR	4	3	4	5	4	4	5	3	4	36
JOHN	5	3	5	5	5	5	⑥	4	4	42
HARRY	4	3	6	⑥	5	4	⑥	3	5	42
+/-										
PETER	6	6	5	⑦	6	6	⑧	5	7	56
RICH	5	4	5	⑦	6	4	6	5	5	47
PAR	4	3	4	5	4	4	5	3	4	36
HANDICAP	7	15	3	11	17	5	1	13	9	
RED COURSE RATING 71.0	331	100	310	462	304	355	484	110	310	2766
DATE:	SCORER:									

To determine your handicap under the Callaway system, do the following: a) find your gross score in the accompanying chart; b) following the chart, deduct the appropriate number of worst holes and make the adjustment listed at the bottom of the chart; c) subtract the resulting "handicap" from your gross score to determine your net score.

Note:
1. No hole should be scored at more than twice its par.
2. Half strokes count as a whole.
3. The seventeenth and eighteenth holes are never deducted.
4. Maximum handicap is 50.
5. In the case of ties lower handicap or adjustment should be given preference.

	10	11	12	13	14	15	16	17	18	IN	TOT	HCP	NET
	515	197	380	390	429	230	481	501	448	3571	7036		
	475	163	351	350	382	197	426	465	428	3237	6366		
	6	18	14	8	16	4	2	10	12				
	5	3	4	4	4	3	4	5	4	36	72		
	(7)	3	4	5	5	4	6	5	5	44	86	11	75
	5	4	5	6	5	4	4	4	4	41	83	9	74
	(7)	4	6	5	(7)	4	5	7	6	51	107	28	79
	(8)	4	4	6	5	4	(7)	5	5	48	95	21	74
	5	3	4	4	4	3	5	5	5	38	74		
	6	18	4	10	16	2	12	8	14				
	420	141	333	299	346	166	398	434	398	2935	5701		

ATTEST:
CHECK TEES PLAYED: ☐ BLUE   ☐ WHITE   ☐ RED

In the sample scorecard, John's gross score was 86. Following the chart, he threw out his two worst holes, a 6 and a 7, for a total of 13 points. He then checked the bottom of the chart under the "86" column and adjusted his "handicap" by deducting 2 points. This gave him a handicap of 11 strokes and a net score of 75.

APPENDIX B
RULES OF GOLF:
DIFFERENCES BETWEEN
STROKE AND MATCH PLAY

In general, the rules of golf are the same for all types of competitions played by golfers everywhere. There are, however, a few exceptions that can be very helpful to the player.

For instance, under the rules of golf if you putt and your ball strikes another ball on the green, you are penalized. However, in Individual Match Play you are not. Therefore, you can request your opponent to leave his ball on the green at any time if you feel this may be advantageous to you. At times this can be very helpful. For example, if you are faced with a fast downhill putt, and your opponent's ball lies beyond the hole, you may want him to leave his ball on the green to stop your ball should it go past the hole.

The rules of golf also state that the player farthest from the hole is the first to play. When playing partners events, however, the side that has the farthest ball from the hole plays first. In some instances it may be helpful to have the closer player of the team go first. For instance, the closer partner may take his shot first in order to help the farther partner judge a course of action, particularly when the farther player has a choice between a safe shot and a riskier one.

Another difference between Match and Stroke Play rules is the handling of a breach of the rules. Stroke Play is scored by the number of strokes a player takes, and thus the penalty for a breach of the rules is always a certain number of penalty strokes. Match Play is played by holes won or lost, and the penalty for a breach of rule is the loss of a hole (except when otherwise specified).

In a Stroke Play tournament a player's handicap is either deducted from his 18-hole score or, in the case of a partners event, his full handicap is spread out as designated in the handicap row of the scorecard. In a Match Play tournament, however, the players in the match stroke off the low-handicap player involved. The difference between the low-handicap player's handicap and those of the other players is allocated to those players according to the hole ratings on the scorecard's handicap row. For example, if one player is a four handicap and his opponent is a seven handicap, the latter player is allotted one stroke on the three toughest holes of the course.

If a Match Play event ends in a tie, a hole-by-hole sudden-death playoff determines the winner. When a Stroke Play event ends in a tie, an 18-hole playoff is suggested to determine the winner (due to time restrictions some other method, such as sudden death or a three-hole playoff, is usually chosen).

In a Stroke Play event the ball must be played until it is holed out. Under the rules of Match Play a player may concede the hole to his opponent if he feels that the player will hole out on the next stroke. A player may concede a hole or the match at any time prior to the conclusion of the hole or the match.

It is recommended that all golfers have a copy of the complete rules of golf to aid in proper understanding and use of the rules.